MAHESHWAR SUTRAS

PRATYAHARAS

Ashwini Kumar Aggarwal

जय गुरुदेव

ॐ

ISBN10:   1-9733-7378-5
ISBN13:   978-1-9733-7378-0

Title Maheshwar Sutras Pratyaharas

31st March 2018 Hanuman Jayanti, Chaitra Poornima
Vasanta Masa, Shukla Paksha, Uttarayana
Vikram Samvat 2075 Virodhakrit, Saka Samvat 1940 Vilambi

Devotees of Sri Sri Ravi Shankar Ashram

The Art of Living Centre
147 Punjabi Bagh, Patiala 147001
Punjab, India

Website https://advaita56.weebly.com/

1st Edition March 2018

जय गुरुदेव

ॐ

Gurudev Sri Sri Ravi Shankar

The one who enlightens

An offering at His Lotus feet

जय गुरुदेव

Acknowledgements

The most wonderful Yoga program at Maitreyi Hall with the Art of Living Sri Sri Yoga teachers for QCI Level2 certification.

Special Thanks

Swamini Brahmaprakasananda, Arsha Vijnana Gurukulam, Nagpur
Pushpa Dikshit, Panini Shodh Sansthan, Bilaspur
Janardana Hegde, Samskrita Bharati, Bangalore

Table of Contents

Preface

At the beginning of the magnificient work the Ashtadhyayi, stand the **14** sutras or aphorisms. The sounds of a ⧗ damru, the symbol of ∞ **infinity**.

Most of us know that sound is connected with the space element, the subtle all pervasive entity that sustains our creation. Sounds are the expression of life, of vitality and of strong connection.

Panini the visionary, the master, the seer begins his magnum opus with such clarity of thought that it resounds till eternity. In one deft movement of his pen, he captures the dynamic rhythms of nature. A budding singer or musician knows very well the octaves, the 7 basic and the 7 upper. The number 14 is also connected to the चतुर्दश भुवनानि, the 14 lokas or planes of existence.

In fact 14 has found parity with चतुर्दशी, the auspicious tithi of Maha Shivaratri. In the modern context, we find the number 14 etched firmly in the Grammy awards and also in Valentine's day.

महा + ईश् + Taddhita affix –> माहेश्वर = Great Benevolence

Pratyahara = Abbreviation = Shorthand = Compact
Thus the 14 aphorisms got the name Maheshwar Sutras.

Blessing

Nataraja is depicted holding a डमरु, the symbol of infinity. When we write the character infinity, it is in the shape of a डमरु । The डमरु generated sound, and that sound produced व्याकरण ।

H H Sri Sri Ravi Shankar
23rd Feb 2017, Maha Shivaratri eve
The Art of Living Bangalore Ashram
https://www.youtube.com/watch?v=MN9a3vqVaZg

Prayer

Traditionally a prayer is chanted before the beginning of any work or study. Since our purpose is study, we have taken a prayer that expresses gratefulness towards our Teacher.

गुरुर्ब्रह्मा गुरुर्विष्णुः गुरुर्देवो महेश्वरः ।
गुरुः साक्षात् परं ब्रह्म तस्मै श्री गुरवे नमः ॥

In Sanskrit, the opening prayer specific to a task is called Mangalacharanam मङ्गलाचरणम् । It helps to focus one's mind on the current topic. Bringing the Mind to The Present Moment.

We recite the famous ode from the School of Yoga Philosophy.

वाक्यकारं वररुचिं भाष्यकारं पतञ्जलिम् ।
पाणिनिं सूत्रकारञ्च प्रणतोऽस्मि मुनित्रयम् ॥
योगेन चित्तस्य पदेन वाचां मलं शरीरस्य च वैद्यकेन ।
योऽपाकरोत्तं प्रवरम मुनीनां पतञ्जलि प्राञ्जलिरानतोऽस्मि ॥

Introduction

In the Grammar we repeatedly come across Sandhi and Samasa. We frequently encounter a change in spelling of words as soon as they are placed in a sentence.

A word when stand-alone or as listed in the dictionary seems to have its spelling altered when it is placed in a sentence. This is due to coalescing or joining, a peculiarity of Sanskrit.

This happens because when a word is spoken aloud singly it will have a different quality. When a sentence is spoken, then due to speed, emphasis, emotion or tone, the distinctiveness of each word may undergo a change. These changes are naturally captured in the Sanskrit Language **even when printing**. Primarily the Sanskrit scriptures and texts were passed on orally from generation to generation. For maintaining precision and accuracy the verses were always chanted in a specific manner.

The science behind the language is given in the Ashtadhyayi, a complete treatise on Sanskrit grammar by the renowned grammarian of yore, Maharishi Panini.

The Ashtadhyayi begins with a code that has come to be known as the Maheshwar Sutras. This code serves two main uses, one of constructing Arrays-of-Letter-Equivalence and the other of introducing the Tags-Indicatory letters.

The Maheshwar Sutras are a careful, systematic, and ingenious rearrangement of the letters of the Sanskrit Alphabet, so that word construction and processing and correct spelling becomes a charm.

Conversely, the Sanskrit Alphabet वर्णमाला can be derived from the Maheshwar Sutras. As we can very well see, there are 42 letters in the माहेश्वरसूत्राणि, 9 vowels and 33 consonants, plus a repetition.

The letter repeated twice is the हकारः
The ह is an aspirate, i.e. mahaprana. It is named thus.

Notice the placement of अ इ उ masculine vowels, and inherent within आ ई ऊ the feminine. This is a simple facet of the Indian tradition, naming the one and assuming the other within. (terms "masculine" and "feminine" are used in the context of "letters and words" to enhance their usability).

Pratyaharas are an ingenious device of the Sanskrit alphabet to allow clustering so that such clusters can be referred to in the Ashtadhyayi.

14 Sutras and 41 Pratyaharas, a mathematical reflection to ensure cyclic redundancy check or error free coding.

The Sanskrit Alphabet

वर्णमाला

ॐ अ आ इ ई उ ऊ ऋ ॠ ऌ ॡ   ए ऐ ओ औ   अं अः

क्	ख्	ग्	घ्	ङ्	The Shiva Sounds
च्	छ्	ज्	झ्	ञ्	
ट्	ठ्	ड्	ढ्	ण्	The Brahma Sounds
त्	थ्	द्	ध्	न्	
प्	फ्	ब्	भ्	म्	The Vishnu Sounds
य् र् ल् व्		श् ष् स्		ह्	
अँ	ळ्		व्ह्		Vedic Sanskrit

Conjunct letters are used frequently क्ष ज्ञ श्र, while
Long ॡ is not noticed in literature. The Sanskrit alphabet is
commonly written without a halant. Consonants cannot be uttered
without a vowel. So in teaching, each consonant is supplied with अ
so that it can be uttered. There are 56 letters in the Vedic Alphabet.

20 Vowels अ आ अ३ इ ई इ३ उ ऊ उ३ ऋ ॠ ऋ३ ऌ ऌ३ ए ऐ ए३ ओ औ ओ३
34 Consonants

क	ख	ग	घ	ङ
च	छ	ज	झ	ञ
ट	ठ	ड	ढ	ण
त	थ	द	ध	न
प	फ	ब	भ	म

य र ल व श ष स   ह and ळ

2 Ayogavahas अं अः

Characteristics of Letters

In the Sanskrit Alphabet, the letters have distinct characteristics.

Simple Vowels - अ आ इ ई उ ऊ ऋ ॠ ऌ

   ह्रस्व Short Vowels अ , इ, उ, ऋ, ऌ

   दीर्घ Long Vowels आ , ई, ऊ , ॠ

Vowels with intrinsic consonant ऋ (अर्) ॠ (आर्) ऌ (अल्)

Compound Vowels सन्ध्यक्षर have been constructed by
   combination and are used independently
   अ + इ = ए
   अ + ए = ऐ = अ + अ + इ
   अ + उ = ओ
   अ + ओ = औ = अ + अ + उ

Semi Vowels अन्तःस्थ standing between vowel and consonant
   य् र् ल् व्

Row class consonants
क् ख् ग् घ् ङ् च् छ् ज् झ् ञ् ट् ठ् ड् ढ् ण् त् थ् द् ध् न् प् फ् ब् भ् म्

Sibilants are called ऊष्म hot श् ष् स्

Aspirate is महाप्राण a release of breath ह्

Homogeneous Letters and Matching

Homogeneous Letters सवर्ण are those that can be considered similar for the purpose of Substitution as per Context.

1.1.9　तुल्यास्यप्रयत्नं सवर्णम् । Letters with similarity of Place and Effort are to be considered homogeneous. *When this is insufficient, then external effort is also considered.*
वा० ऋॢवर्णयोर्मिथः सावर्ण्यं वाच्यम् । Letters ऋ and ॡ are to be considered homogeneous.

1.1.10　नाज्झलौ । However a Vowel and a Consonant are not, even if both have same Place and Internal Effort.

1.1.49　षष्ठी स्थाने योगा ।

1.1.50　स्थानेऽन्तरतमः ।

1.1.52　अलोऽन्त्यस्य ।

1.1.68　स्वं रूपं शब्दस्याशब्दसंज्ञा । In using the Ashtadhyayi, when a *word* is under-consideration-for-an-operation, then the-individual-letters-of-that *word* are to be seen and then operated upon.
Also, if a *word* **is a technical definition in the Ashtadhyayi,** then its meaning is to be applied without splitting it into individual letters.

1.1.69　अणुदित्सवर्णस्य चाप्रत्ययः । उदित् letters refer to their

1.1.70　तपरस्तत्कालस्य ।

1.1.71　आदिरन्त्येन सहिता ।

Lets us examine some of the homogeneous letters.

Gutturals कुँ = कवर्ग are considered homegeneous to one another. Within the gutturals, we have attributes, namely Hard, Soft, Nasal and Prana.

> For matching Hard letters क् , ख् are homogeneous
> For matching Soft letters ग् , घ् are homogeneous
> For matching MahaPrana letters ख् , घ् are homogeneous

Similarly for the other row class consonants.

Nasals find match relevance when they become Anusvara. Then changes occur based on corresponding row nasal.
> e.g. न् after changing to ं can further change to one of ङ् , ञ् , ण् , न् , म्

The sibilants do not have a class, so their matching is based on place of utterance.
> palatal श् would match palatals   च , छ , ज , झ्
> cerebral ष् would match cerebrals ट , ठ , ड , ढ
> dental स् would match dentals   त , थ , द , ध्

> for some matching, we consider hardness and prana
> palatal श् would match palatal छ्
> cerebral ष् would match cerebral ठ्
> dental स् would match dental थ्

> for some matching, we consider prana alone
> palatal श् would match palatal झ्
> cerebral ष् would match cerebral ढ्
> dental स् would match dental ध्

The semi vowels have matching nasals.
> palatal य has matching nasal यँ
> dental ल has matching nasal लँ
> cerebral व has matching nasal वँ
> for repha there isn't any.

The Aspirate हकार doesn't have a direct match, but by Prana we have पूर्वसवर्ण match. Thus ह् may change to corresponding MahaPrana letter
> घ् , झ् , ढ् , ध् , भ्

What came First?

In the Sanskrit classes, sometimes a question is asked –

What came First?
Did the Maheshwar Sutras originate before the Sanskrit Alphabet or vice versa?

It is good to understand the context. The Sanskrit Language has been spoken since a long long time. It has been in usage ever since mankind started to communicate. Whereas Maharishi Panini is dated to be circa 600 BCE, and is credited for establishing the rules and logic and methods *inherent* in the construction of words; verbs and nouns.

Which means that Panini formulated the laws whereby the linguistics, syntax, semantics and spellings could be correctly arrived at.

So the Sanskrit Language and the Sanskrit Alphabet certainly predates the Maheshwar Sutras.

The Maheshwar Sutras are the techniques that Panini was bestowed on by grace, so that he could describe the grammar.

Synonyms of Maheshwar Sutra

In the course of time, many adjectives made their way to refer to the Maheshwar Sutras. Some of the more common are

1. माहेश्वरसूत्र	Maheshwar Sutra	Origin from the sounds of the damru
2. अक्षरसमाम्नाय	the totality of the sacred indestructible	All that is divine and eternal
3. शिवसूत्र	Shiva Sutra	Synonym for Maheshwar
4. वर्णसमाम्नाय	Homogeneity of Sacred Letters	Stating the sacred letters and their similarities
5. प्रत्याहारसूत्र	Pratyahara Sutra	Abbreviation or compactness or cluster

Reference from Verses

1. माहेश्वसूत्र   2. अक्षरसमाम्नाय

येनाक्षरसमाम्नायमधिगम्य महेश्वरात् ।
कृत्स्नं व्याकरणं प्रोक्तं तस्मै पाणिनये नमः ॥

येन् अक्षरसमाम्नायम् अधिगम्य महेश्वरात् ।
कृत्स्नं व्याकरणं प्रोक्तं तस्मै पाणिनये नमः ॥

येन् by whom अक्षरसमाम्नायम् the totality of the sacred indestructible
अधिगम्य becomes practical for learning महेश्वरात् from the great Lord
कृत्स्नं complete व्याकरणं grammar प्रोक्तं taught तस्मै to him पाणिनये
Panini नमः Salutation

3. शिवसूत्र

नृत्तावसाने नटराजराजो ननाद ढक्कां नवपञ्चवारम् ।
उद्धर्तुकामः सनकादिसिद्धानेतद्विमर्शे शिवसूत्रजालम् ॥

नृत्त अवसाने नटराजराजः ननाद ढक्काम् नवपञ्च वारम् ।
उद्धर्तु कामः सनकादिसिद्धान् एतत् विमर्शे शिवसूत्रजालम् ॥

नृत्त dance अवसाने at culmination नटराजराजः Lord of dance ननाद made
a loud sound ढक्काम् damru नवपञ्च fourteen वारम् times
उद्धर्तु to liberate कामः desiring सनकादिसिद्धान् Sanaka etc. virtuous and
qualified men एतत् this विमर्शे in hindsight शिवसूत्रजालम् an auspicious
collection of verses

Etymology of Māheśvarāṇi

A simple व्युत्पत्ति etymology

माहेश्वराणि सूत्राणि = The Maheshwar Sutras
The Sutras originating from Maheshwar

माहेश्वराणि [n1/3]	सूत्राणि [n1/3]
adjective	substantive (noun)

माहेश्वराणि => विग्रह = महेश्वरात् आगतानि = arisen from Maheshwar

To make such words we employ a कृदन्त affix
Particulary the अण् affix is used in the sense of ततः आगतः arising
from

महेश्वर stem + अण् kRit Affix = माहेश्वर stem

It will decline as फल शब्दः in neuter
since in this context it is used as an adjective to सूत्र शब्दः

सूत्राणि = The Sutras (plural because these are 14 in number)

माहेश्वराणि = neuter case 1/3 प्रथमा बहुवचनम्

Etymology of Pratyāhāra

The word pratyahara has become quite famous from the text on yoga philosophy named the Yogasutras of Patanjali. In the normal context प्रत्याहार implies a restraint, a discipline or a moderation.

Similarly the meaning has been extended in the sense of grammar to imply a clustering or a compacting. Specifically to denote an abbreviation or an array.

प्रत्याहार = प्रति upasarga + आङ् particle + ह dhatu + घञ् affix

Dhatu 899 हृञ् हरणे = to take away, to attract, to steal

kṚit Affix घञ् is commonly employed to make a noun

Pratyahara = Constriction of excessiveness = Abbreviation

Maheshwar Sutras

माहेश्वराणि सूत्राणि Encompasses sounds that are the foundation of the Devanagari Alphabet. Attributed to Maharishi Panini circa 600 BC.

1	अ इ उ	ण्	All vowels = अच्
2	ऋ ऌ	क्	Simple vowels = अक्
3	ए ओ	ङ्	Diphthongs = एच्
4	ऐ औ	च्	Semivowels = यण्
5	ह य व र	ट्	All consonants = हल्
6	लँ	ण्	ल्+अँ, No nasal for र्
7	ञ म ङ ण न	म्	5th of row = Nasals = ञम्
8	झ भ	ञ्	4th of row = झष्
9	घ ढ ध	ष्	are all soft consonants
10	ज ब ग ड द	श्	3rd of row = जश् (soft)
11	ख फ छ ठ थ च ट त	व्	1st and 2nd of row = खय्
12	क प	य्	are all hard consonants
13	श ष स	र्	Sibilants (hard) = शर्
14	ह	ल्	Aspirate is soft

Consonants have been written with अकार solely for enunciation.

But in लँण् there is an anunasika Tag अँ and a consonant Tag ण् ।

From these 14 Sutras are cognised the 41 Pratyaharas (Arrays).

With inputs from later grammarians, the number of pratyaharas has been revised to 41+3 + 2 = 46.

There are 9+33+1(+13) = 56 letters in the Sanskrit alphabet as succintly depicted here. *Including a repeated Tag ण् total is 57.*

Maheshwar Sutras IAST Transliteration

Transliteration using ISO 15919 standard

1	अ इ उ	ण्	a i u	Ṇ
2	ऋ ऌ	क्	r̥ l̥	K
3	ए ओ	ङ्	ē ō	Ṅ
4	ऐ औ	च्	ai au	C
5	ह य व र	ट्	ha ya va ra	T
6	ऌँ	ण्	lă	Ṇ
7	ञ म ङ ण न	म्	ña ma ṅa ṇa na	M
8	झ भ	ञ्	jha bha	Ñ
9	घ ढ ध	ष्	gha ḍha dha	Ṣ
10	ज ब ग ड द	श्	ja ba ga ḍa da	Ś
11	ख फ छ ठ थ च ट त	व्	kha pha cha ṭha tha ca ṭa ta	V
12	क प	य्	ka pa	Y
13	श ष स	र्	śa ṣa sa	R
14	ह	ऌ्	ha	L

Consonants have been written with vowel "a" solely for enunciation. But in ऌँण् there is an anunasika Tag अँ and a consonant Tag ण् ।

Maheshwar Sutras as Chanted

Chant aloud these aphorisms for a deep healing effect.

अ इ उ ण्	a i uṇ
ऋ ऌ क्	ṛ ḷk
ए ओ ङ्	ē ōṅ
ऐ औ च्	ai auc
ह य व र ट्	ha ya va raṭ
ल ँ ण्	lãṇ
ञ म ङ ण न म्	ña ma ṅa ṇa nam
झ भ ञ्	jha bhañ
घ ढ ध ष्	gha ḍha dhaṣ
ज ब ग ड द श्	ja ba ga ḍa daś
ख फ छ ठ थ च ट त व्	kha pha cha ṭha tha ca ṭa tav
क प य्	ka pay
श ष स र्	śa ṣa sar
ह ल्	hal

Traditionally the Indian texts were written thus.

अइउण् । ऋऌक्। एओङ्। ऐऔच् । हयवरट्। लँण् । ञमङणनम् । झभञ् । घढधष् । जबगडदश् । खफछठथचटतव् । कपय् । शषसर् । हल् ॥ इतिप्रत्याहारसूत्राणि ॥

24

Maheshwar Sutras showing attributes

For clarity in understanding we may rewrite the sutras with spacing

1	अ इ उ	ण्	simple vowels
2	ऋ ऌ	क्	Intrinsic consonant vowels
3	ए ओ	ङ्	Compound vowels
4	ऐ औ	च्	Compounded Compound vowels
Vowel consonant boundary			
5	ह य व र	ट्	Aspirate and semi-
6	ल ̐	ण्	vowels
Row class consonants			
7	ञ म ङ ण न	म्	Nasals 5th of class
8	झ भ	ञ्	Soft aspirated 4th of class
9	घ ढ ध	ष्	
10	ज ब ग ड द्	श्	Soft un-aspirated 3rd of class
11	ख फ छ ठ थ		Hard aspirated 2nd of class
	च ट त	व्	Hard un-aspirated 1st of class
12	क प	य्	Hard un-aspirated 1st of class (: , ×)
13	श ष स	र्	Hard aspirated sibilants hot
14	ह	ऌ	Soft Aspirate

Tags used are the nasals ङ् ञ् ण् म् , semi vowels य् र् ऌ व् , 1st of row hard consonants क् च् ट् and sibilants श् ष् । Notice that these tags are the ones that are crisp and distinct in enunciation.

25

Maheshwar Sutras Number Magic

A profound mathematics has been encoded by Panini as noticed.

अ इ उ ण् । ऋ ल़ क् । ए ओ ङ् । ऐ औ च् ।
ह य व र ट् । ल़ ण् । ञ म ङ ण न म् ।
झ भ ञ् । घ ढ ध ष् । ज ब ग ड द श् ।
ख फ छ ठ थँ च ट त व् । क प य् ।
श ष स र् । ह ल् ।

From these 14 Sutras are cognised the 41 Pratyaharas. A mathematical inversion 1 4 - 4 1. The famous Indian festival dedicated to Lord Shiva, Maha Shivratri is observed on a चतुर्दशी the 14th night of the waning moon.

pi to *five* places: 3.14159 shows up the number 14.

Silicon's atomic number is 14; it has 14 protons and a melting point of 1414 °C. Silicon finds significant use in the manufacture of computer chips, electronic circuits and *mobiles, the modern day language of our planet.*

Count of letters = 9+33+1(+13) = 56 letters. The Sanskrit alphabet contains 56 letters. *Not including the repeated* ण् *Tag.*

Count of distinct vowels = 9 and count of consonants = 33 is also clearly seen. *Not including the repeated* ह *letter.*

Oldest scripture RigVeda begins with अकारः and contains हकारः ।
अग्निमीळे पुरोहितं यज्ञस्य देवमृत्विजम् ।
होतारं रत्नधातमम् ॥ Rigveda 1.1.1.1

Question: Purpose of the repeated ह letter?

A proposed answer is to indicate the presence of ayogavaha letters not explicit here but commonly used in literature. Anusvara, visarga, ardha visarga (jihvamuliya, upadhmaniya). Also it definitely serves a technical point related to the pratyaharas as used in the Ashtadhyayi. Finally it is a mangalacharanam letter as it denotes प्राण = महाप्राण = Life Force = Breath = Aspirate

Question: Purpose of the repeated ण् Tag?

A proposed answer is that it is for Mangalacharanam as it is at the ending in the word नारायण Narayan.

A recent study by linguists also shows that this method of arranging the Shiva Sutras and using Pratyaharas is applicable to other languages, e.g. German.

Pratyaharas

Panini has used Pratyaharas as a shorthand notation for keeping his Ashtadhyayi compact. Pratyaharas condense various letters of the alphabet into a single syllable. These consist of 2 letters, *or 3 letters when consonant-beginning simply for the purpose of enunciation the vowel अकार: gets added*. The second or last letter is usually a Tag letter.

The first letter specifies an alphabet subset, or a sutra, or a ganapatha. The second letter specifies the closing Tag of another. By this, it represents the entire sequence of letters contained in both and everything in-between.

Not to be confused with the Pratyahara or pragmatic-use-of-senses from Yogasutras of Patanjali

Maheshwar Sutras = माहेश्वरसूत्राणि = माहेश्वराणि सूत्राणि = composed by Lord Maheshwar = Lord Shiva = शिवसूत्राणि
Not to be confused with the Shiva Sutras or aphorisms of Advaita Vedanta that were revealed by Lord Shiva to Sage Vasugupta.

माहेश्वरसूत्राणि = प्रत्याहारसूत्राणि since the Pratyaharas are primarily formed from these. A Pratyahara refers to a commonality or a common property.

A famous karika states that the rishis Sanaka etc. heard the damru of Lord as it sounded 9+5 i.e. 14 times
नत्तावसाने नटराजराजो ननाद ढक्कां नवपञ्च वारम् ।
उद्धर्तु कामः सनकादि सिद्धान् एतद् विमर्शे शिव–सूत्र–जालम् ॥
The Lord's dance culminates in the loud sounding of his damru fourteen times, as He wills to enlighten the qualified men, Sanaka etc. In hindsight these sounds are a group of meaningful verses.

The Maheshwar Sutras are a group of letters ending in a Tag. There are 43 letters in all, with the हकारः repeated twice. Thus we have 9 vowels + 33 consonants + 1 repeated consonant = 43 letters.

14 sutras and 41 pratyaharas
14 bones of the face

The sequence of letters in the Maheshwar Sutras is a kind of multi-tasking coding. In the वर्णमाला we see क ख ग घ to specify the standard sequence of guttural letters, whereas in the माहेश्वरसूत्राणि we see these four letters spread over four Sutras with other letters in between. The reason is that माहेश्वरसूत्राणि is hinting us regarding many other attributes that are also common to these letters.

Similarly note that the वर्णमाला gives semivowels in the sequence य र ल व, whereas माहेश्वरसूत्राणि gives it as य व र ल to indicate a one-to-one relation between the earlier mentioned vowels इ उ ऋ ऌ which we notice when doing Samprasarana or यण् Sandhi.

The familiar concepts of computer programming viz. "classes", "inheritance", "variables" and "constants" is thus inherent in माहेश्वरसूत्राणि । Right at the beginning of the Ashtadhyayi!

And the same style of multi-threading, super-computing, elegant-coding is followed throughout the Ashadhyayi of Panini.

Excerpts from Mahabhashya

The Mahabhashya written in the form of a dialogue with questions and answers and commentary, says in its

1st Ahnika named पस्पशाह्निक

Chapter 1, Pada 1

Bhashya line 144 अथ किमर्थो वर्णानामुपदेशः ?

Vartika 19 वृत्तिसमवायार्थ उपदेशः ।

Bhashya line 145 वृत्तिसमवायार्थो वर्णानामुपदेशः०

Vartika 20 अनुबन्धकरणार्थश्च ।

Bhashya line 146 अनुबन्धकरणार्थश्च वर्णानामुपदेशः । अनुबन्धानासङ्ख्यामि इति । न ह्यनुपदिश्य वर्णाननुबन्धाः शक्या आसङ्कुम् । स एष वर्णानामुपदेशो वृत्तिसमवायार्थश्च अनुबन्धकरणार्थश्च । वृत्तिसमवायश्चानुबन्धकरणं च प्रत्याहारार्थम् । प्रत्याहारो वृत्त्यर्थः ।

2nd Ahnika प्रत्याहाराह्निक

अ इ उ ण् ॥१॥

Vartika 1 अकारस्य विवृतोपदेश आकारग्रहणार्थः ।

Bhashya line 1 अकारस्य विवृतोपदेशः कर्तव्यः । किं प्रयोजनम् ? आकारग्रहणार्थः०

Maheshwar Sutras w.r.t. Pratyaharas

The one-to-one relation

SN	Sutras	Pratyaharas	Count
1	अ इ उ ण्	अण्	1
2	ऋ ऌ क्	अक् इक् उक्	3
3	ए ओ ङ्	एङ्	1
4	ऐ औ च्	अच् इच् एच् ऐच्	4
5	ह य व र ट्	अट्	1
6	ल ँ ण्	अण् इण् यण् (र्ँ)	3
7	ञ म ङ ण न म्	अम् यम् ङम् (ञम्)	3
8	झ भ ञ्	यञ्	1
9	घ ढ ध ष्	झष् भष्	2
10	ज ब ग ड द श्	अश् हश् वश् झश् जश् बश्	6
11	ख फ छ ठ थँ च ट त व्	छव् (खँ)	1
12	क प य्	यय् मय् झय् खय् (चय्) (जय्)	4
13	श ष स र्	यर् झर् खर् चर् शर्	5
14	ह ळ्	अल् हल् वल् रल् झल् शल्	6
		Basic Count of Pratyaharas =	41
	Extended Count 41 + ③ = 44, with later grammarians = 46		

According to Mahabhashya, the ayogavaha characters anusvara, visarga, ardha visarga and yama are to be included in अट् , शर् ।
The long vowels आ , ई , ऊ , ॠ get included in अक् , अच् ।

31

Tags and Pratyaharas

Sometimes we need to look it up precisely
Tags and Pratyaharas **in sequence** of the Shiva Sutras

1	ण्	अण्
2	क्	अक् इक् उक्
3	ङ्	एङ्
4	च्	अच् इच् एच् ऐच्
5	ट्	अट्
6	ण् , अँ	अण् इण् यण् रँ
7	म्	अम् यम् जम् ङम्
8	ञ्	यञ्
9	ष्	झष् भष्
10	श्	अश् हश् वश् झश् जश् बश्
11	व् , अँ	छव् खँ
12	य्	यय् जय् मय् झय् खय् चय्
13	र्	यर् झर् खर् चर् शर्
14	ल्	अल् हल् वल् रल् झल् शल्

Notes

Anunasika Tag अँ from लँ in a Vartika is not counted by most.

Anunasika Tag अँ from थँ to make Pratyahara खँ is a later entry.

Pratyahara जय् denotes all the 25 row class consonants, and is also a later addition for teaching purposes that does not directly find use in word construction.

Pratyaharas Expanded

The letters of each Pratyahara must be clear. Notice that the Consonants are with a **halant** in the Pratyaharas.

1	अ इ उ	ण्	अण्	अ , इ , उ also आ , ई , ऊ
2	ऋ ऌ	क्	अक्	अ , इ , उ , ऋ , ऌ also आ , ई , ऊ , ऋ
			इक्	इ , ई , उ , ऊ , ऋ , ॠ , ऌ
			उक्	उ , ऊ , ऋ , ॠ , ऌ
3	ए ओ	ङ्	एङ्	ए , ओ
4	ऐ औ	च्	अच्	अ, आ, इ, ई, उ, ऊ, ऋ, ॠ, ऌ, ए ओ ऐ औ
			इच्	इ , ई , उ , ऊ , ऋ , ॠ , ऌ , ए , ओ , ऐ ,औ
			एच्	ए , ओ , ऐ , औ
			ऐच्	ऐ , औ
5	ह य व र	ट्	अट्	अ , आ , इ , ई , उ , ऊ , ऋ , ॠ , ऌ , ए , ओ , ऐ , औ , ह् , य् , व् , र्
6	लँ	ण्	अण्	अ , आ , इ , ई , उ , ऊ , ऋ , ॠ , ऌ , ए , ओ , ऐ , औ , ह् , य् , व् , र् , ऌ
			इण्	इ , ई , उ , ऊ , ऋ , ॠ , ऌ , ए , ओ , ऐ , औ , ह् , य् , व् , र् , ऌ
			यण्	य् , व् , र् , ऌ
			रँ	र् , ऌ
7	ञ म ङ ण न	म्	अम्	अ, आ, इ, ई, उ, ऊ, ऋ, ॠ, ऌ, ए, ओ, ऐ, औ, ह्, य्, व्, र्, ऌ, ञ्, म्, ङ्, ण्, न्
			यम्	य् , व् , र् , ऌ , ञ् , म् , ङ् , ण् , न्
			ञम्	ञ् , म् , ङ् , ण् , न्
			ङम्	ङ् , ण् , न्
8	झ भ	ञ्	यञ्	य् , व् , र् , ऌ , ञ् , म् , ङ् , ण् , न् , झ् भ्

9	घढध ष्	झष्	झ्, भ्, घ्, ढ्, ध्
		भष्	भ्, घ्, ढ्, ध्
10	जबगडद श्	अश्	अ, आ, इ, ई, उ, ऊ, ऋ, ॠ, ऌ, ए, ओ, ऐ, औ, ह्, य्, व्, र्, ल्, ञ्, म्, ङ्, ण्, न्, झ्, भ्, घ्, ढ्, ध्, ज्, ब्, ग्, ड्, द्
		हश्	ह्, य्, व्, र्, ल्, ञ्, म्, ङ्, ण्, न्, झ्, भ्, घ्, ढ्, ध्, ज्, ब्, ग्, ड्, द्
		वश्	व्, र्, ल्, ञ्, म्, ङ्, ण्, न्, झ्, भ्, घ्, ढ्, ध्, ज्, ब्, ग्, ड्, द्
		झश्	झ्, भ्, घ्, ढ्, ध्, ज्, ब्, ग्, ड्, द्
		जश्	ज्, ब्, ग्, ड्, द्
		बश्	ब्, ग्, ड्, द्
11	खफछठथँ चटत व्	खँ	ख्, फ्, छ्, ठ्, थ्
		छव्	छ्, ठ्, थ्, च्, ट्, त्
12	कप य्	यय्	य्, व्, र्, ल्, ञ्, म्, ङ्, ण्, न्, झ्, भ्, घ्, ढ्, ध्, ज्, ब्, ग्, ड्, द्, ख्, फ्, छ्, ठ्, थ्, च्, ट्, त्, क्, प्
		जय्	ञ्, म्, ङ्, ण्, न्, झ्, भ्, घ्, ढ्, ध्, ज्, ब्, ग्, ड्, द्, ख्, फ्, छ्, ठ्, थ्, च्, ट्, त्, क्, प्
		मय्	म्, ङ्, ण्, न्, झ्, भ्, घ्, ढ्, ध्, ज्, ब्, ग्, ड्, द्, ख्, फ्, छ्, ठ्, थ्, च्, ट्, त्, क्, प्
		झय्	झ्, भ्, घ्, ढ्, ध्, ज्, ब्, ग्, ड्, द्, ख्, फ्, छ्, ठ्, थ्, च्, ट्, त्, क्, प्
		खय्	ख्, फ्, छ्, ठ्, थ्, च्, ट्, त्, क्, प्
		चय्	च्, ट्, त्, क्, प्

34

13	श ष स	रॢ	यरॢ	य, व, र, ल, ञ, म, ङ, ण, न, झ, भ, घ, ढ, ध, ज, ब, ग, ड, द, ख, फ, छ, ठ, थ, च, ट, त, क, प, श, ष, स
			झरॢ	झ, भ, घ, ढ, ध, ज, ब, ग, ड, द, ख, फ, छ, ठ, थ, च, ट, त, क, प, श, ष, स
			खरॢ	ख, फ, छ, ठ, थ, च, ट, त, क, प, श, ष, स
			चरॢ	च, ट, त, क, प, श, ष, स
			शरॢ	श, ष, स
14	ह	लॢ	अलॢ	Complete Alphabet = All Letters
			हलॢ	क ख ग घ ङ च छ ज झ ञ ट ठ ड ढ ण त थ द ध न प फ ब भ म य र ल व श ष स ह
			वलॢ	व, र, ल, ञ, म, ङ, ण, न, झ, भ, घ, ढ, ध, ज, ब, ग, ड, द, ख, फ, छ, ठ, थ, च, ट, त, क, प, श, ष, स, ह
			रलॢ	र, ल, ञ, म, ङ, ण, न, झ, भ, घ, ढ, ध, ज, ब, ग, ड, द, ख, फ, छ, ठ, थ, च, ट, त, क, प, श, ष, स, ह
			झलॢ	झ, भ, घ, ढ, ध, ज, ब, ग, ड, द, ख, फ, छ, ठ, थ, च, ट, त, क, प, श, ष, स, ह
			शलॢ	श, ष, स, ह

Pratyaharas Named

The pratyaharas can be named based on quality.

1	अ इ उ	ण्	अण्	Simple Vowels short and long *but without the vowels with an inherent consonant*
2	ऋ ऌ	क्	अक्	**Simple Vowels short and long**
			इक्	Samprasarana Vowels or **Vowels that take Guna**
			उक्	
3	ए ओ	ङ्	एङ्	Part of Guna Letters
4	ऐ औ	च्	अच्	**All Vowels**
			इच्	
			एच्	Compound Vowels
			ऐच्	Part of Vriddhi Letters
5	ह य व र	ट्	अट्	Letters that take नो णः । e.g. रामेन to रामेण
6	लँ	ण्	अण्	Vowels, Semi Vowels, Aspirate
			इण्	Vowels except अवर्ण, Semi Vowels
			यण्	**All Semi Vowels,** यण् Sandhi letters
			रँ	Letters that are inherent in the Special Vowels ऋ , ऌ
7	ञ म ङ ण न	म्	अम्	Vowels, Semi Vowels, Nasals and Aspirate
			यम्	Semi Vowels and Nasals
			ञम्	5th of row class consonants = Nasals
			ङम्	
8	झ भ	ञ्	यञ्	
9	घ ढ ध	ष्	झष्	4th of row row class consonants
			भष्	

10	ज ब ग ड द	श्	अश्	All Vowels and Soft Consonants
			हश्	**All Soft Consonants**
			वश्	
			झश्	4th and 3rd of row
			जश्	**3rd of row class consonants**
			बश्	
11	ख फ छ ठ थँ चटत	व्	खँ	2nd of row class consonants
			छव्	
12	क प	य्	यय्	Semi Vowels and Mutes
			ञय्	**All row class consonants = Mutes**
			मय्	
			झय्	4th , 3rd , 2nd and 1st of row
			खय्	2nd and 1st of row = Hard = Surds
			चय्	**1st of row class consonants**
13	श ष स	र्	यर्	All consonants except Aspirate
			झर्	Sibilants, 4th, 3rd, 2nd and 1st of row
			खर्	All Hard consonants
			चर्	
			शर्	**Sibilants = Hot**
14	ह	ल्	अल्	**Complete Alphabet = All Letters**
			हल्	**All Consonants**
			वल्	Letters that specify वलादि सेट् Roots
			रल्	
			झल्	All consonants except nasals
			शल्	Sibilants and Aspirate

Pratyaharas Named and Expanded

The letters of the Pratyaharas have been slightly rearranged to match with the वर्णमाला Sanskrit Alphabet, for clarity in use.

अण्	Simple Vowels short and long *but without the vowels with an inherent consonant*	अ , आ , इ , ई , उ , ऊ
अक्	**Simple Vowels**	अ , आ , इ , ई , उ , ऊ , ऋ , ॠ , ऌ
इक्	Samprasarana Vowels or **Vowels that take Guna**	इ , ई , उ , ऊ , ऋ , ॠ , ऌ
उक्		उ , ऊ , ऋ , ॠ , ऌ
एङ्	Part of Guna Letters	ए , ओ
अच्	**All Vowels**	अ , आ , इ , ई , उ , ऊ , ऋ , ॠ , ऌ , ए , ऐ, ओ, औ
इच्	All Vowels except अवर्ण guttural	इ , ई , उ , ऊ , ऋ , ॠ ,ऌ,ए ,ऐ ,ओ, औ
एच्	Compound Vowels	ए , ऐ , ओ, औ
ऐच्	Part of Vriddhi Letters	ऐ, औ
अट्	Letters that take नो णः । e.g. रामेन to रामेण	अ , आ , इ , ई , उ , ऊ , ऋ , ॠ , ऌ , ए , ऐ, ओ, औ । ह् । य्, व्, र्
अण्	All Vowels, Semi Vowels and Aspirate	अ , आ , इ , ई , उ , ऊ , ऋ , ॠ , ऌ , ए , ऐ, ओ, औ । ह् । य्, व्, र्, ल्
इण्	Vowels except अवर्ण, Semi Vowels and Aspirate	इ , ई , उ , ऊ , ऋ , ॠ , ऌ , ए , ऐ, ओ , औ, ह् , य्, व्, र्, ल्
यण्	**All Semi Vowels,** यण् Sandhi letters	य्, र्, ल्, व्
र्ँ	Letters that are inherent in the Special Vowels ऋ , ऌ	र्, ल्
अम्	Vowels, Semi Vowels, Nasals and Aspirate	अ, आ, इ, ई, उ, ऊ, ऋ, ॠ, ऌ, ए, ऐ, ओ, औ । य्,र्, ल्, व्। ङ्, ञ्, ण्, न्, म्। ह्

38

यम्	Semi Vowels and Nasals	य्, र्, ल्, व् । ङ्, ञ्, ण्, न्, म्
ञम्	5th of row class consonants = Nasals	ङ्, ञ्, ण्, न्, म्
ङम्		ङ्, ण्, न्
यञ्		य्, र्, ल्, व् । ङ्, ञ्, ण्, न्, म् । झ्, भ्

झष् — 4th of row

				घ्	
				झ्	
				ढ्	
				ध्	
				भ्	

भष्	4th of row except palatal	घ्, ढ्, ध्, भ्

अश् — All Vowels and Soft Consonants

		ग्	घ्	ङ्	अ आ इ ई
		ज्	झ्	ञ्	उ ऊ ऋ ॠ
		ड्	ढ्	ण्	ऌ
		द्	ध्	न्	ए ऐ ओ औ
		ब्	भ्	म्	
य्	र्	ल्	व्		
				ह्	

हश् — All Soft Consonants

		ग्	घ्	ङ्
		ज्	झ्	ञ्
		ड्	ढ्	ण्
		द्	ध्	न्
		ब्	भ्	म्
य्	र्	ल्	व्	
				ह्

वश्			ग्	घ्	ङ्
			ज्	झ्	ञ्
			ड्	ढ्	ण्
			द्	ध्	न्
			ब्	भ्	म्
		र्	ल्	व्	
झश्	4th and 3rd of row		ग्	घ्	
			ज्	झ्	
			ड्	ढ्	
			द्	ध्	
			ब्	भ्	
जश्	3rd of row class consonants		ग्		
			ज्		
			ड्		
			द्		
			ब्		
बश्	3rd of row except palatal ज्	ग् , ड् , द् , ब्			
खँ	2nd of row class consonants	ख् , फ् , छ् , ठ् , थ्			
छव्		च् छ् ट् ठ् त् थ्			

यय्	Semi Vowels and Mutes	क्	ख्	ग्	घ्	ङ्
		च्	छ्	ज्	झ्	ञ्
		ट्	ठ्	ड्	ढ्	ण्
		त्	थ्	द्	ध्	न्
		प्	फ्	ब्	भ्	म्
		य्	र्	ल्	व्	
जय्	**All row class consonants = Mutes**	क्	ख्	ग्	घ्	ङ्
		च्	छ्	ज्	झ्	ञ्
		ट्	ठ्	ड्	ढ्	ण्
		त्	थ्	द्	ध्	न्
		प्	फ्	ब्	भ्	म्
मय्	Mutes except palatal ञ्	क्	ख्	ग्	घ्	ङ्
		च्	छ्	ज्	झ्	
		ट्	ठ्	ड्	ढ्	ण्
		त्	थ्	द्	ध्	न्
		प्	फ्	ब्	भ्	म्
झय्	4th , 3rd , 2nd and 1st of row	क्	ख्	ग्	घ्	
		च्	छ्	ज्	झ्	
		ट्	ठ्	ड्	ढ्	
		त्	थ्	द्	ध्	
		प्	फ्	ब्	भ्	

खय्	2nd and 1st of row = Hard = Surds	क्	ख्			
		च्	छ्			
		ट्	ठ्			
		त्	थ्			
		प्	फ्			
चय्	1st of row class consonants	क्				
		च्				
		ट्				
		त्				
		प्				
यर्	All consonants except Aspirate	क्	ख्	ग्	घ्	ङ्
		च्	छ्	ज्	झ्	ञ्
		ट्	ठ्	ड्	ढ्	ण्
		त्	थ्	द्	ध्	न्
		प्	फ्	ब्	भ्	म्
		य्	र्	ल्	व्	
		श्	ष्	स्		
झर्	Sibilants, 4th, 3rd, 2nd and 1st of row	क्	ख्	ग्	घ्	
		च्	छ्	ज्	झ्	
		ट्	ठ्	ड्	ढ्	
		त्	थ्	द्	ध्	
		प्	फ्	ब्	भ्	
		श्	ष्	स्		

खर्	All Hard consonants	क्	ख्				
		च्	छ्				
		ट्	ठ्				
		त्	थ्				
		प्	फ्				
		श्	ष्	स्			
चर्	Sibilants and 1st of row	क्					
		च्					
		ट्					
		त्					
		प्					
		श्	ष्	स्			
शर्	Sibilants = Hot	श् , ष् , स्					
अल्	Complete Alphabet = All Letters = Vowels and Consonants	अ आ इ ई उ ऊ ऋ ॠ ल़ ए ऐ ओ औ।					
		क्	ख्	ग्	घ्	ङ्	
		च्	छ्	ज्	झ्	ञ्	
		ट्	ठ्	ड्	ढ्	ण्	
		त्	थ्	द्	ध्	न्	
		प्	फ्	ब्	भ्	म्	
		य्	र्	ल्	व्		
		श्	ष्	स्	ह्		

हल्	All Consonants	क्	ख्	ग्	घ्	ङ्
		च्	छ्	ज्	झ्	ञ्
		ट्	ठ्	ड्	ढ्	ण्
		त्	थ्	द्	ध्	न्
		प्	फ्	ब्	भ्	म्
		य्	र्	ल्	व्	
		श्	ष्	स्	ह्	
वल्	Letters that specify वलादि सेट् Roots	क्	ख्	ग्	घ्	ङ्
		च्	छ्	ज्	झ्	ञ्
		ट्	ठ्	ड्	ढ्	ण्
		त्	थ्	द्	ध्	न्
		प्	फ्	ब्	भ्	म्
			र्	ल्	व्	
		श्	ष्	स्	ह्	
रल्		क्	ख्	ग्	घ्	ङ्
		च्	छ्	ज्	झ्	ञ्
		ट्	ठ्	ड्	ढ्	ण्
		त्	थ्	द्	ध्	न्
		प्	फ्	ब्	भ्	म्
			र्	ल्		
		श्	ष्	स्	ह्	

झल्	All consonants except nasals or semi vowels	क्	ख्	ग्	घ्	
		च्	छ्	ज्	झ्	
		ट्	ठ्	ड्	ढ्	
		त्	थ्	द्	ध्	
		प्	फ्	ब्	भ्	
		श्	ष्	स्	ह्	
शल्	Sibilants and Aspirate	श्, ष्, स्, ह्				

Alphabetical Tags and Pratyaharas

Looking at these from different angles can open up a greater understanding.

Tags alphabetical अँ क् ङ् च् ञ् ट् ण् ण् म् य् र् ल् व् श् ष्

			अँ
क्			ङ्
च्			ञ्
ट्			ण् , ण्
			म्
य्	र्	ल्	व्
श्	ष्		

Pratyaharas alphabetical
अक्-अच्-अट्-अण्-अण्-अम्-अल्-अश्-इक्-इच्-इण्-उक्-एङ्-एच्-ऐच्-खँ-खय्-खर्-ङम्-चय्-चर्-छव्-जश्-झय्-झर्-झल्-झश्-झष्-ञम्-जय्-बश्-भष्-मय्-यञ्-यण्-यम्-यय्-यर्-रँ-रल्-वल्-वश्-शर्-शल्-हल्-हश्

अक् अच् अट् अण् अण् अम् अल् अश् इक् इच् इण् उक्
एङ् एच् ऐच्
खँ खय् खर् ङम्
चय् चर् छव् जश् झय् झर् झल् झश् झष् ञम् जय्
बश् भष् मय्
यञ् यण् यम् यय् यर् रँ रल् वल् वश्
शर् शल्
हल् हश्

Maheshwar Sutras Pratyaharas Ashtadhyayi

The one-to-one relation

SN	Sutras	Pratyaharas	Ashtadhyayi
1	अ इ उ ण्	अण्	1.1.51
2	ऋ ऌ क्	अक्, इक्, उक्	6.1.101, 1.1.3, 4.1.6
3	ए ओ ङ्	एङ्	6.1.94
4	ऐ औ च्	अच्, इच्, एच्, ऐच् 1.1.64, 6.3.68, 6.1.78, 1.1.1	
5	ह य व र ट्	अट्	8.4.63
6	लँ ण्	अण्, इण्, यण्, रँ 1.1.69, 8.3.57, 6.1.77, Vartika 1.1.51	
7	ञ म ङ ण न म्	अम्, यम्, ङम्, जम् 8.3.6, 8.4.64, 8.3.32, Unadi 1.114	
8	झ भ ञ्	यञ्	7.3.101
9	घ ढ ध ष्	झष्, भष्	8.2.37
10	ज ब ग ड द श्	अश्, हश्, वश्, झश्, जश्, बश् 8.3.17, 6.1.114, 7.2.8, 8.4.53, 8.2.39 8.2.37	
11	ख फ छ ठ थँ च ट त व्	छव्, खँ	8.3.7, Later Grammarian
12	क प य्	यय्, ञय्, मय्, झय्, खय्, चय् 8.4.58, Later Grammarian, 8.3.33, 8.4.62, 8.3.6, Vartika 8.4.48	
13	श ष स र्	यर्, झर्, खर्, चर्, शर् 8.4.45, 8.4.65, 8.4.55, 8.4.54, 8.3.36	
14	ह ल्	अल्, वल्, रल्, झल्, शल्, हल् 1.1.65, 6.1.66, 1.2.26, 8.2.26, 3.1.45, 1.1.7	

The Mahabhashya of Patanjali discusses some nuances of grammer as it enumerates the first eight Shiva Sutras in its 2nd Ahnika.

Pratyaharas w.r.t. Ashtadhyayi

A thorough understanding is the key to a strong foundation. This table gives a handy reference.

SN	Sutra	Pratyahara	Ashtadhyayi
1	अ इ उ ण्	अण् 1.1.51 उरण् रपरः । उः अण् रपरः । अण्[1/1]	
2	ऋ ऌ क्	अक्, इक्, उक्	
	6.1.101 अकः सवर्णे दीर्घः । अकः is 5/1 form of stem अक् 1.1.3 इको गुणवृद्धी । इकः is 6/1 form of stem इक् 4.1.6 उगितश्च । उगि तः च । उगि is 7/1 of stem उक् after sandhi		
3	ए ओ ङ्	एङ् 6.1.94 एङि पररूपम् । एङि [7/1] of stem एङ्	
4	ऐ औ च्	अच्, इच्, एच्, ऐच् 1.1.64 अचोऽन्त्यादि टि । अचः [5/1] of अच् 6.3.68 इच एकाचोऽम्प्रत्ययवच्च । इचः [6/1] of इच् 6.1.78 एचोऽयवायावः । एचः [6/1] of एच् 1.1.1 वृद्धिरादैच् । वृद्धिः आत्-ऐच् [1/1] ।	
5	ह य व र ट्	अट् 8.4.63 शश्छोऽटि । शः छः अटि । अटि [7/1]	
6	लँ ण्	अण्, इण्, यण्, रँ	
	1.1.69 अणुदित् सवर्णस्य चाप्रत्ययः । अण्–उदित् सवर्णस्य चाप्रत्ययः । 8.3.57 इण्कोः । इण्–कोः । 6.1.77 इको यणचि । इकः यण् [1/1] अचि । 1.1.51 उरण् रपरः । उः अण् रँ–परः । बालमनोरमा० अत्र रँ इति प्रत्याहारो विवक्षितः ।		

7	ञ म ङ ण न म्	अम् , यम् , ञम् , ङम्
		8.3.6 पुमः ख्य्यम्परे । पुमः खयि अम्–परे ।
		8.4.64 हलो यमां यमि लोपः । यमि [7/1] form of stem यम्
		Unadi 1.114 ञमन्ताड् ङः । अम् अन्तात् ङः ।
		8.3.32 ङमो ह्रस्वादचि ङमुण्नित्यम् । ङमः 5/1 form of stem ङम्
8	झ भ ञ्	यञ् 7.3.101 अतो दीर्घो यञि । यञि [7/1]
9	घ ढ ध ष्	झष् , भष्
		8.2.37 एकाचो बशो भष् झषन्तस्य स्ध्वोः ।
		एकाचो बशो भष्[1/1] झष्–अन्तस्य स्ध्वोः ।
10	ज ब ग ड द श्	अश् , हश् , वश् , झश् , जश् , बश्
		8.3.17 भोभगोअघोअपूर्वस्य योऽशि । अशि [7/1]
		6.1.114 हशि च । हशि [7/1] of stem हश्
		7.2.8 नेड् वशि कृति । वशि [7/1] of stem वश्
		8.4.53 झलां जश् झशि । झशि [7/1] of stem झश्
		8.2.39 झलां जशोऽन्ते । जशः [6/1] of stem जश्
		8.2.37 एकाचो बशो भष् झषन्तस्य स्ध्वोः । बशः [6/1]
11	ख फ छ ठ थँ च ट त व्	छव् खँ
		8.3.7 नश्छव्यप्रशान् । नः छवि अप्रशान् । छवि [7/1]
		Some grammarians have included खँ
12	क प य्	यय् , ञय् , मय् , झय् , खय् , चय्
		8.4.58 अनुस्वारस्य ययि परसवर्णः । ययि [7/1]
		ञय् are the Row Class Consonants, specified by some later grammarians
		8.3.33 मय उञो वो वा । मयः [5/1]
		8.4.62 झयो होऽन्यतरस्याम् । झयः [5/1]
		7.4.61 शर्पूर्वाः खयः । खयः [1/3]
		8.4.48 नादिन्याक्रोशे पुत्रस्य । वा॰ चयो द्वितीयाः शरि पौष्करसादेरिति वाच्यम् । चयः [6/1]

13	श ष स र्	यर् , झर् , खर् , चर् , शर्
		8.4.45 यरोऽनुनासिकेऽनुनासिको वा । यरः 6/1
		8.4.65 झरो झरि सवर्णे । झरः 6/1 झरि 7/1
		8.4.55 खरि च । खरि 7/1
		8.4.54 अभ्यासे चर्च । अभ्यासे चर् च । चर् 1/1
		8.3.36 वा शरि । शरि 7/1
14	ह ळ	अल् , हल् , वल् , रल् , झल् , शल्
		1.1.65 अलोऽन्त्यात् पूर्व उपधा । अलः 5/1
		1.1.7 हलोऽनन्तराः संयोगः । हलः 1/3
		हकारः of Pratyahara हल् is from शिवसूत्र ह य व र ट्
		6.1.66 लोपो व्योर्वलि । वलि 7/1
		1.2.26 रलो व्युपधाद्धलादेः संश्र । रलः 5/1
		8.2.26 झलो झलि । झलः 5/1 झलि 7/1 ।
		3.1.45 शल इगुपधादनिटः क्सः । शलः 5/1

41 Pratyaharas from Ashtadhyayi Sutras, One Pratyahara अम् from Unadi patha, Two Pratyaharas रैँ , चय् from Vartikas, Two Pratyaharas जय् , खँ added by later grammarians = 46 total count.

णकार Tag is repeated in अ इ उ ण् and लँ ण् ।
Keep in mind the Tags from Shiva Sutras in sequence
ण् क् ङ् च् ट् अँ ण् म् ञ् ष् श् व् य् र् ल् for the discussion
There is the अण् Pratyahara using णकार from अ इ उ ण् and there are अण् , इण् , यण् Pratyaharas using णकार from लँ ण् ।

Keep in mind the Pratyaharas from Shiva Sutras in sequence
अण् अक् इक् उक् एङ् अच् इच् एच् ऐच् अट् अण् इण् यण् रैँ अम् यम् अम् ङम् यञ् झष् भष् अश् हश् वश् झश् जश् बश् छव् खँ यय् जय् मय् झय् खय् चय् यर् झर् खर् चर् शर् अल् हल् वल् झल् शल् for the discussion
हकार Letter is repeated in ह य व र ट् and ह ल् ।
Both हश् and हल् Pratyaharas use हकार from ह य व र ट् ।
The हकार of ह य व र ट् is used in Pratyaharas अट् अण् इण् अम् अश् हश्
The हकार of ह ल् is used for Pratyaharas वल् रल् झल् शल्

Coincidentally हल् is both the name of a Shiva Sutra and also a Pratyahara. The 14th Shiva Sutra is हल् and there is a हल् Pratyahara made from हकार of 5th Shiva Sutra.

The Pratyahara अल् that includes all letters of the alphabet has the letter हकार repeated, to signify that the ayogavahas – anusvara, visarga, ardha visarga and yama – are also part of the Alphabet.

Pratyahara Charts Examined

When an Ashtadhyayi Sutra ordains a letter replacement आदेश, then we see how the Pratyahara Arrays work to determine the closest replacement for the स्थानी ।

Notice that some letters in the charts are either redundant or serve no technical usage.

E.g. क्+क्=>क्+क् ॥

  क्+ख्=>क्+ख् ॥

Some situations from the charts may not be encountered in the language at all.

E.g. हृ+क् ॥

These are what we call boundary conditions or never-used-conditions during computer programming and logic coding.

At the same time, such statements serve a key role in keeping the code compact and error free, while maintaining lucidity and clarity.

01 Pratyahara aṇ

1	अ इ उण्	अण्

1.1.51 उरण् रपरः । उ: 6/1 अण् 1/1 रपरः 1/1 ।

When ऋवर्ण is to be replaced by an अण् letter, Then रेफ gets attachedto the अण् letter. Here उ: is genitive 6/1 of stem ऋ ।
बालमनोरमा० अत्र रँ इति प्रत्याहारो विवक्षितः । The repha is qualified to be the pratyahara रँ, so it includes the letters र् and ल् ।

1.1.9 तुल्यास्यप्रयत्नं सवर्णम् । Similarity of place and effort are the criteria to establish homogeneity of letters.
वा० ऋकारॡकारयोः सवर्णसंज्ञा वाच्या । The Vartika extends ऋवर्ण to include ॡ ।

1.1.3 इको गुणवृद्धी । The इक् letters will undergo Guna or Vriddhi. Traditionally अवर्ण qualifies to be nearest to ऋवर्ण in matters of Guna or Vriddhi.

7.1.100 ऋत इद्धातोः । A Root ending in ऋकार gets इकारादेश ।

4.1.115 मातुरुत्सङ्ख्यासंभद्रपूर्वायाः । Stem मातृ gets उकारादेश when used in numerical collections.

ऋवर्ण स्थानी m1/1	अण् letter आदेशः m1/1	after addendum Guna । Vriddhi	
ऋ	अ , आ , इ , ई , उ , ऊ	अर्	आर्
ॠ		अर्	आर्
ॢ		अल्	आल्

1.1.3 After addendum shows Guna or Vriddhi of ऋवर्ण ।

7.1.100 In case इ has been ordered as the replacement for ऋ , then इर् will actually be the replacement.

4.1.115 When उ is ordered to be the replacement for ऋ , then उर् is the substituend.

02 Pratyahara ak

2	ऋ ल क्	अक्, इक्, उक्

6.1.101 अकः सवर्णे दीर्घः । अकः is 5/1 form of stem अक्

When अक् letter is followed by a homogeneous अच् letter, then both get replaced by a homogeneous long vowel.

अक् letter स्थानी m1/1		सवर्ण अच् letter वर्तमाने m7/1		सवर्ण long vowel आदेशः m1/1
अ	आ	अ	आ	आ
इ	ई	इ	ई	ई
उ	ऊ	उ	ऊ	ऊ
ऋ	ॠ	ऋ	ॠ	ॠ
ऌ		ऌ		ॠ

03 Pratyahara ik

1.1.3 इको गुणवृद्धी । इकः is 6/1 form of stem इक्

The इक् letters will undergo Guna or Vriddhi.

इक् letter स्थानी m1/1		Guna letter आदेशः m1/1		Vriddhi letter आदेशः m1/1	
इ	ई	ए		ऐ	
उ	ऊ	ओ		औ	
ऋ	ॠ	अ		आ	
ऌ		अ		आ	

04 Pratyahara uk

4.1.6 उगितश्च । उगि तः च । उगि is 7/1 of stem उक् after sandhi
Stem ending in उक् letter(उ, ऊ, ऋ , ॠ , ऌ) gets ङीप् affix in feminine.

05 Pratyahara ēṅ

3	ए ओ ङ्	एङ्

6.1.94 एङि पररूपम् । एङि 7/1 of stem एङ्

When Upasarga ending in अवर्ण is followed by a Root beginning with an एङ् letter, Then both get replaced by the एङ् letter.

Upasarga ending in अवर्ण = स्थानी m1/1	Root beginning with एङ् letter=वर्तमाने m7/1		Single Substituend आदेश: m1/1
अप	2	एध	ए
अव	121	ओखृ	ओ
आ	179	एजृ	ए
उप	234	एजृ	ए
परा	267	एठ	ए
प्र	454	ओणृ	ओ
	618	एषृ	ए
	1542	ओलडि	ओ

4	ऐ औ च्	अच् , इच् , एच् , ऐच्

1.1.64 अचोऽन्त्यादि टि । अच: [5/1] of अच्

In an entity, the final अच् letter and consonants-if-any following the final अच् letter are named टि ।

3.4.79 टित आत्मनेपदानां टेरे । In the Lakaras having टकार as Tag, when doing an Atmanepada derivation, then the टि portion of those Atmanepada affixes gets replaced by एकार ।

Thus even though the name टि can theoretically be given to the suitable portion of any entity, it has an effect only in the scope of Ashtadhyayi Sutras 3.4.79 and 3.4.80 । So we see Prakriti Atmanepada Affixes त आताम् झ being replaced by ते आते अन्ते ।

e.g. consider various entities like Root, Verb, Noun, Affix.

Some entities		Final अच् letter		टि portion of entity	
भू		उ		उ	
भवति		इ		इ	
भूतः		अ		अः	
एधते		ए		ए	
आताम्		आ		आम्	
अग्निचित्		इ		इत्	

07 Pratyahara ic

6.3.68 इच एकाचोऽम्प्रत्ययवच्च । इचः 6/1 of इच्

When a monosyllabic entity ending in इच् letter is followed by an entity ending in खित् , Then the augment अम् gets added. This अम् behaves as the accusative case 2/1 affix अम् ।

08 Pratyahara ēc

6.1.78 एचोऽयवायावः । एचः 6/1 of एच्

When एच् letter is followed by an अच् letter, Then अय् अव् आय् आव् are the corresponding replacements to the एच् letter.

एच् letter स्थानी m1/1		अच् letter=वर्तमाने m7/1	Substituend आदेश: m1/1	
ए		अ , आ , इ , ई , उ , ऊ ,	अय्	
ओ		ऋ , ॠ , ऌ , ए , ऐ , ओ ,	अव्	
ऐ		औ	आय्	
औ			आव्	

57

09 Pratyahara aic

1.1.1 वृद्धिरादैच् । वृद्धिः आत्-ऐच् [1/1] ।

The letters आत् and ऐच् are called Vriddhi.

1.1.70 तपरस्तत्कालस्य । When तकार is prefixed or affixed to a letter, then that specific letter having that particular length of time alone is indicated.

Thus the Vriddhi letters are आ , ऐ and औ ।

10 Pratyahara aṭ

5	ह य व र ट्	अट्

8.4.63 शश्छोऽटि । शः छः अटि । अटि [7/1]

When झय् letter is followed by शकारः and शकारः is followed by an अट्
letter, then Optionally शकारः is replaced by छकारः ।

वा॰ छत्वम्मीति वक्तव्यम् । छत्वम् अमि इति वक्तव्यम् । Vartika says that
instead of अट् letters, it happens for अम् letters.

झय् letter = वर्तमाने [m7/1]	शकारः = स्थानी [m1/1]	अट् letter = वर्तमाने [m7/1]	Substituend आदेशः[m1/1]
झ,भ , घ , ढ , ध , ज , ब , ग , ड , द , ख , फ , छ , ठ , थ , च , ट , त , क , प	श्	अ , आ , इ , ई , उ , ऊ , ऋ , ॠ , ल , ए , ओ , ऐ , औ , ह् , य् , व् , र्	छ्
e.g. वाक् + शेते = वाक् + श् + एते => वाक्छेते । पक्षे वाक्शेते । By Vartika even तत् + श्लोकेन = तत् + श् + लोकेन => तत् छ्लोकेन । (By further Sandhi तच्छ्लोकेन)			

11 Pratyahara lăṇ

6	लँ ण्	अण् , इण् , यण् , रँ

1.1.69 अणुदित् सवर्णस्य चाप्रत्ययः । अण्–उदित् सवर्णस्य चाप्रत्ययः ।
Letters of अण् and Letters of उदित् वर्ण indicate themselves and all
their similar letters, except when these are used as Affixes.

अण् letters	उदित् letters
अ , आ , इ , ई , उ , ऊ , ऋ , ॠ , ल , ए , ओ , ऐ ,	कुँ = क ख ग घ ङ चुँ = च छ ज झ ञ

औ, ह्, य्, व्, र्, ल्	टुँ = ट् ठ् ड् ढ् ण्
	तुँ = त् थ् द् ध् न्
	पुँ = प् फ् ब् भ् म्

12 Pratyahara iṇ

8.3.57 इण्कोः । इण्–कोः ।

This is a governing rule that says that sutras in its scope will work for इण् letters and for कवर्ग letters.

e.g. 8.3.59 आदेशप्रत्यययोः । Changes सकार to षकार when सकार is preceded by an इण् letter or by a कवर्ग letter.

इण् letter वर्तमाने m7/1	कवर्ग letter वर्तमाने m7/1	स्थानी m1/1	Substituend आदेशः m1/1
इ , ई , उ , ऊ , ऋ , ॠ , ऌ , ए , ऐ , ओ , औ , ह् , य् , व् , र् , ल्	क् , ख् , ग् , घ् , ङ्	स्	ष्
इण् e.g. करोषि (ओ + स्) => (ओ + ष्) । भविष्यति (इ + स्) => (इ + ष्) । कवर्ग e.g. रोक्ष्यति (क् + स्) => (क् + ष्) ॥			

61

13 Pratyahara yaṇ

6.1.77 इको यणचि । इकः यण् [1/1] अचि ।

When इक् letter is followed by अच् letter, then इक् letter gets replaced by corresponding यण् letter. Note that in cases when इक् letter is followed by सवर्ण इक् letter, then a subsequent rule 6.1.101 overrides.

इक् letter स्थानी [m1/1]		अच् letter वर्तमाने [m7/1]	Substituend यण् letter आदेशः [m1/1]
इ	ई	अ , आ , (इ , ई , उ , ऊ ,	य्
उ	ऊ	ऋ , ॠ , ऌ) , ए , ऐ , ओ ,	व्
ऋ	ॠ	औ	र्
ऌ			ल्
हि + आत्मनः => ह् य् आत्मनः => ह्यात्मनः ।			

14 Pratyahara ra̐

1.1.51 उरण् रपरः । उः अण् रँ–परः । When ऋवर्ण is to be replaced by an अण् letter, Then रेफ gets attachedto the अण् letter. Here उः is genitive 6/1 of stem ऋ ।

बालमनोरमा॰ अत्र रँ इति प्रत्याहारो विवक्षितः । The repha is qualified to be the pratyahara रँ, so it includes the letters र् and ल् ।

15 Pratyahara am

| 7 | ञ म ङ ण न म् | अम् , यम् , ञम् , ङम् |

8.3.6 पुमः खय्यम्परे । पुमः खयि अम्–परे ।

When entity पुम् is followed by खय् letter that is further followed by अम् letter, Then रँ is the replacement for मकारः । By further processing the उ gets nasalised to उँ or उं and रँ to सकारः ।

पुम् entity	खय् letter	अम् letter	Substituend रँ
स्थानी m1/1	वर्तमाने m7/1	वर्तमाने m7/1	आदेशः m1/1
पुम्	ख, फ, छ, ठ, थ, च, ट्, त्, क्, प्	अ, आ, इ, ई, उ, ऊ, ऋ, ॠ, ल्, ए, ओ, ऐ, औ, ह्, य्, व्, र्, ल्, ञ्, म्, ङ्, ण्, न्	पुरँ
e.g. पुम् क् आ मा => पुरँ क् आ मा । Further पुँस्कामा , पुंस्कामा ।			

16 Pratyahara yam

8.4.64 हलो यमां यमि लोपः । यमि [7/1] form of stem यम्

When हल् letter is followed by यम् letter that is further followed by यम् letter, then the preceding यम् letter is Optionally dropped.

हल् letter वर्तमाने [m7/1]	यम् letter स्थानी [m1/1]	यम् letter वर्तमाने [m7/1]	आदेशः [m1/1]
Any consonant	य्, व्, र्, ल्, ञ्, म्, ङ्, ण्, न्	य्, व्, र्, ल्, ञ्, म्, ङ्, ण्, न्	लोपः of यम् letter
e.g. श् य् य् आ => श्य्या or शय्या । आदित्यः or आदित्य्यः ।			

64

17 Pratyahara ñam

Unadi 1.114 अमन्ताड् ङः । अम् अन्तात् ङः ।
An entity ending in अम् letter gets the ङ Affix.

1.3.7 चुटू । In the Upadesha, the initial चु = चवर्ग letter and the initial
टु = टवर्ग letter is a Tag, hence dropped. However for this Unadi
Sutra, बहुलवचनात् इत् संज्ञा निषेधः । Thus दण्डः , अण्डः ।

18 Pratyahara ṅam

8.3.32 ङमो ह्रस्वादचि ङमुण्नित्यम् । ङमः 5/1 form of stem ङम्

When a word ending in ङम् letter preceded by a short vowel is followed by an अच् letter, Then the अच् letter takes a ङमुट् augment always, i.e. a doubling of the ङम् letter occurs.

Word ending in ङम् letter preceded by a short vowel वर्तमाने m7/1		अच् letter स्थानी m1/1	ङमुट् आगमः m1/1
अ , इ , उ , ऋ , ळ	ङ , ण , न्	Any vowel	ङुट् , णुट् , नुट्
e.g. प्रत्यङ् + आस्ते => प्रत्यङ्ङास्ते । वण्णास्ते , कुर्वन्नास्ते ।			

19 Pratyahara yañ

8	झ भ ञ्	यञ्

7.3.101 अतो दीर्घो यञि । यञि [7/1]

Anga ending in अकार takes दीर्घ replacement when it is followed by a Sarvadhatuka affix that begins with a यञ् letter (मिप्, वस्, मस्). Famous examples are the first person singular, dual and plural Verbs of Present Tense.

भव + मिप् लट् i/1 => भव् अ + मि => 7.3.101 => भव् आ मि = भवामि ।

20 Pratyahara jhaṣ

Pratyahara झष् stands for 4th of row class consonants. These are soft aspirated.

9	घ ढ ध ष्	झष् , भष्

8.2.40 झषस्तथोर्द्धोऽधः । झषः 5/1

When a झष् letter is followed by a तकार or थकार, Then the तकार or थकार get धकारादेश । However it does not happen for Root दुधाञ् । e.g. Root दुह् + लट् iii/1 => दोग्धि / दुग्धे । बुध + क्त => बुद्धः ।

21 Pratyahara bhaṣ

Pratyahara भष् stands for 4th of row except झकार । These are soft aspirated.

8.2.37 एकाचो बशो भष् झषन्तस्य स्ध्वोः ।

एकाचो बशो भष्1/1 झष्–अन्तस्य स्ध्वोः ।

For a Root ending in a झष् letter, to its monosyllabic portionthat begins with a बश् letter, there is substituted a भष् letter. In the case of end of word or when facing सकार or ध्व of an Affix.

बश् letter स्थानी m1/1	झष् letter वर्तमाने m7/1	वर्तमाने m7/1	भष् letter आदेशः m1/1
ब् , ग् , ड् , द्	झ् , भ् , घ् , ढ् , ध्	पदान्ते , स् , ध्व	भ् , घ् , ढ् , ध्
e.g. बुध + लृट् iii/1 => बुध + स्यते => भुध् + स्यते । Further processing gives final Verb as भोत्स्यते ।			
दुह् => धोक्ष्यति , धोक्ष्यते , धोक्षि , धुक्षे , धुग्ध्वे , अधोक् , अधुग्ध्वम् ।			

22 Pratyahara aś

Pratyahara अश् consists of the alphabet except for hard consonants and sibilants.

10	ज ब ग ड द श्	अश् , हश् , वश् , झश् , जश् , बश्

8.3.17 भोभगोअघोअपूर्वस्य योऽशि । अशि 7/1

The यकार is substituted for repha of रँ preceded by भो , भगो , अघो or अवर्ण, When रँ is followed by an अश् letter.

भो , भगो , अघो or अवर्ण + रूँ + अश् => अकार + य् + अश् ।

23 Pratyahara haś

Pratyahara हश् consists of all the soft consonants.

6.1.114 हशि च । हशि $^{7/1}$ of stem हश्

The उकार is substituted for repha of रँ preceded by अकार, When रँ is followed by a हश् letter.

अकार + रँ + हश् => अकार + उ + हश् ।

24 Pratyahara vaś

Pratyahara वश् consists of soft consonants except य् , व् ।

7.2.8 नेड् वशि कृति । वशि ⁷/¹ of stem वश्

A कृत् affix having an initial वश् letter does not allow इट् augment.
e.g. Root ईश् => ईश्वरः ।

25 Pratyahara jhaś

Pratyahara झश् consists of 3rd and 4th of row class consonants.

8.4.53 झलां जश् झशि । झशि 7/1 of stem झश्

In a sandhi अपदान्त situation, When a झल् letter is followed by a झश् letter, Then it gets replaced by a जश् letter.

This is one of the most common Sandhi during Verb conjugation and Noun declination.

झल् letter स्थानी m1/1				झश् letter वर्तमाने m7/1			जश् letter आदेश: m1/1	
क्	ख्	ग्	घ्	ग्	घ्	3rd and 4th of row, soft aspirated	ग्	3rd of row, soft unaspirated
च्	छ्	ज्	झ्	ज्	झ्		ज्	
ट्	ठ्	ड्	ढ्	ड्	ढ्		ड्	
त्	थ्	द्	ध्	द्	ध्		द्	
प्	फ्	ब्	भ्	ब्	भ्		ब्	
श्	Palatal						ज्	
ष्	Cerebral						ड्	
स्	Dental						द्	
ह्	Guttural						ग्	

e.g. बुध् + त = > बोद्धा । Similarly दोग्धा । Some more processing is also involved to make this final word.

26 Pratyahara jaś

Pratyahara झश् consists of 3rd of row class consonants. These are soft unaspirated.

8.2.39 झलां जशोऽन्ते । जश: 6/1 of stem जश्

In a sandhi पदान्त situation, When a झल् letter is followed by a virama, Then it gets replaced by a जश् letter.

This is a common Sandhi during Verb conjugation and Noun declination, and also in sentences.

झल् letter स्थानी m1/1					virama वर्तमाने m7/1	जश् letter आदेश: m1/1	
क्	ख्	ग्	घ्		At a word end, or between two words in a sentence	ग्	3rd of row, soft unaspirated
च्	छ्	ज्	झ्			ज्	
ट्	ठ्	ड्	ढ्			ड्	
त्	थ्	द्	ध्			द्	
प्	फ्	ब्	भ्			ब्	
श्	Palatal					ज्	
ष्	Cerebral					ड्	
स्	Dental					द्	
ह्	Guttural					ग्	
e.g. वाक् + अत्र => वाग् अत्र ।							

73

27 Pratyahara baś

Pratyahara बश् consists of 3rd of row except जकार । These are soft unaspirated.

8.2.37 एकाचो बशो भष् झषन्तस्य स्ध्वोः । बशः [6/1]

For a Root ending in a झष् letter, to its monosyllabic portionthat begins with a बश् letter, there is substituted a भष् letter. In the case of end of word or when facing सकार or ध्व of an Affix.

बश् letter स्थानी [m1/1]	झष् letter वर्तमाने [m7/1]	वर्तमाने [m7/1]	भष् letter आदेशः [m1/1]
ब्, ग्, ड्, द्	झ्, भ्, घ्, ढ्, ध्	पदान्ते , स् , ध्व	भ्, घ्, ढ्, ध्

11	ख फ छ ठ थँ च ट त वॣ	छव् खँ

8.3.7 नश्छव्यप्रशान् । नः छवि अप्रशान् । छवि 7/1

For the final नकार of a word, रँ is substituted, when नकार is followed by a छव् letter that is attached to an अम् letter. However it does not apply to the word प्रशान् ।

स्थानी m1/1	छव् letter + अम् letter वर्तमाने m7/1		Substituend आदेश: m1/1
Final न्	छ् , ठ् , थ् , च् , ट् , त्	vowel, semi vowel, nasal	रँ
e.g. भवान् + चलति => भवान् + च् अ लति => भवारँ + चलति । Further processing gives final word as भवाँश्चलति or भवांश्चलति ।			

29 Pratyahara khă̐

Some grammarians have included pratyahara खँ to collect the 2nd of row class consonants. These are hard aspirated. Also called surds.

It is a good method of teaching the grammar.

Consider the usage for Pratyahara चय्
8.4.48 नादिन्याक्रोशे पुत्रस्य ।
वा० चयो द्वितीयाः शरि पौष्करसादेरिति वाच्यम् । चयः 6/1
Vartika qualifies that in the opinion of the grammarian Paushkara, When चय् letter is followed by शर् letter, Then चय् letter is replaced by its corresponding 2nd of class row consonant. This is Optional. We may use the खँ pratyahara here.

12	क प य्	यय् , जय् , मय् , झय् , खय् , चय्

8.4.58 अनुस्वारस्य ययि परसवर्णः । ययि [7/1]

When Anusvara is followed by a यय् letter, Then anusvara is replaced by corresponding परसवर्ण letter.

स्थानी [m1/1]	यय् letter वर्तमाने [m7/1] Consonants except for sibilants and aspirate					Substituend आदेशः [m1/1] Corresponding परसवर्ण
अनुस्वार ंं	क्	ख्	ग्	घ्	ङ्	ङ्
	च्	छ्	ज्	झ्	ञ्	ञ्
	ट्	ठ्	ड्	ढ्	ण्	ण्
	त्	थ्	द्	ध्	न्	न्
	प्	फ्	ब्	भ्	म्	म्
	य्	र्	ल्	व्		ंं

Root अकि => अंक् => अङ्क् ।
Root अजि => अंज् => अञ्ज् ।
Root अठि => अंठ् => अण्ठ् ।
Root अदि => अंद् => अन्द् ।
Root अबि => अंब् => अम्ब् ।
संरक्षते => संरक्षते । no change

31 Pratyahara ñay

Pratyahara ञय् gives all the Row Class Consonants. These are 25 in number. All the mutes or contacted letters. This Pratyahara has been made by some later grammarians for the purpose of teaching, but it does not find direct application in word processing.

Perhaps the sutra
8.4.58 अनुस्वारस्य ययि परसवर्णः ।
could have been अनुस्वारस्य ञयि परसवर्णः ??

क्	ख्	ग्	घ्	ङ्
च्	छ्	ज्	झ्	ञ्
ट्	ठ्	ड्	ढ्	ण्
त्	थ्	द्	ध्	न्
प्	फ्	ब्	भ्	म्

8.3.33 मय उञो वो वा । मयः 5/1

When a मय् letter is followed by the particle उञ् preceding an अच्
letter, Then Optionally the उञ् takes वकारादेश ।

1.1.17 उञः ।

Particle उञ् is defined as प्रगृह्यम् so it will not take vowel Sandhi.

मय् letter वर्तमाने m7/1					उञ् particle स्थानी m1/1	अच् letter वर्तमाने m7/1	Substituend आदेशः m1/1
क्	ख्	ग्	घ्	ङ्	उ	any vowel अ आ इ ई उ ऊ ऋ ॠ ऌ ए ऐ ओ औ	व्
च्	छ्	ज्	झ्				
ट्	ठ्	ड्	ढ्	ण्			
त्	थ्	द्	ध्	न्			
प्	फ्	ब्	भ्	म्			
Row consonants except ञ्							
e.g. शम् उ अस्तु => शम् व् अस्तु => शम्वस्तु । पक्षे शमु अस्तु ।							

33 Pratyahara jhay

8.4.62 झयो होऽन्यतरस्याम् । झयः ^{5/1}

When a झय् letter is followed by हकार , Then Optionally the हकार gets पूर्वसवर्णादेश ।

झय् letter वर्तमाने m7/1					हकार स्थानी m1/1	Substituend पूर्वसवर्ण आदेशः m1/1
क्	ख्	ग्	घ्	Row consonants except nasals	हू	घ्
च्	छ्	ज्	झ्			झ्
ट्	ठ्	ड्	ढ्			ढ्
त्	थ्	द्	ध्			ध्
प्	फ्	ब्	भ्			भ्
e.g. वाक् + हसति => वाक् घसति । By further processing वाग्घस्ति । पक्षे वाग्हसति ।						

80

34 Pratyahara khay

7.4.61 शर्पूर्वाः खयः । शर्-पूर्वाः खयः 1/3

Of a Reduplicate, When consisting of a शर् letter attached to a खय्
letter and other letters, Then only such खय् letter is retained and
other consonants are dropped.

वा॰ खर्पूर्वाः खय इति वक्तव्यम् । Of a Reduplicate, When consisting of a
खर् letter attached to a खय् letter and other letters, Then only such
खय् letter is retained and other consonants are dropped.

Reduplicate consisting of शर् + खय् letter + any more consonant and vowel स्थानी m1/1				Retention of खय् letter and लोपः m1/1 of other consonants
श् , ष् , स् Sibilant	क् ख् च् छ् ट् ठ् त् थ् प् फ्	Hard conson ant except Sibilant	Any more letters	Only single खय् letter retained, other consonants dropped
e.g. Root श्च्युतिर् सन् affix => श्च्युत् सन् => श्च्युत् श्च्युत् इ स ति => श् च् उ त् श्च्युत् इ स ति => Retention of such खय् letter => चु श्च्युत् इषति => चुश्च्योतिषति । Root ष्ठा + सन् affix => स्था स्था स ति => था स्था षति । By further processing तिष्ठासति ।				

81

35 Pratyahara cay

8.4.48 नादिन्याक्रोशे पुत्रस्य ।

In a sentence when the meaning conveyed is of anger or revulsion, When stem पुत्र is followed by stem आदिन् , Then reduplication does not occur for पुत्र ।

वा० चयो द्वितीयाः शरि पौष्करसादेरिति वाच्यम् । चयः 6/1

Vartika qualifies that in the opinion of the grammarian Paushkara, When चय् letter is followed by शर् letter, Then चय् letter is replaced by its corresponding 2nd of class row consonant. This is Optional.

We may use the खँ pratyahara here.

चय् letter स्थानी m1/1	शर् letter वर्तमाने m7/1	Substituend आदेशः m1/1
क् च् ट् त् प् 1st of class Row consonant	श् , ष् , स् Sibilant	ख् छ् ठ् थ् फ् 2nd of Row class consonant खँ
e.g. वथ्सः । पक्षे वत्सः ॥ अखरम् । पक्षे अक्षरम् ॥ अफ्सरा । अप्सरा ॥		

13	श ष स र्	यर् , झर् , खर् , चर् , शर्

8.4.45 यरोऽनुनासिकेऽनुनासिको वा । यर: 6/1

Final यर् letter is Optionally changed to its corresponding row class Nasal, When followed by Nasal.

यर् letter Consonants except Aspirate स्थानी m1/1	Nasal वर्तमाने m7/1	Substituend आदेश: m1/1
क् ख् ग् घ् ङ् च् छ् ज् झ् ञ् ट् ठ् ड् ढ् ण् त् थ् द् ध् न् प् फ् ब् भ् म् य् र् ल् व् श् ष् स्	ङ् Nasal ञ् ण् न् म्	ङ् Nasal ञ् ण् न् म्
e.g. वाक् नयति => वाङ् नयति । पक्षे वाग् नयति । अग्निचित् नयति => अग्निचिन् नयति । पक्षे अग्निचिद् नयति ।		

8.4.65 झरो झरि सवर्णे । झरः 6/1 झरि 7/1

When a हल् letter is followed by a झर् letter that is further followed by a सवर्ण झर् , Then Optionally there is elision of the preceding झर् letter.

हल् letter वर्तमाने m7/1	झर् letter स्थानी m1/1				सवर्ण झर् letter वर्तमाने m7/1				Preceding झर् letter लोपः m1/1
Any consonant	क्	ख्	ग्	घ्	क्	ख्	ग्	घ्	हल् + झर्
	च्	छ्	ज्	झ्	च्	छ्	ज्	झ्	
	ट्	ठ्	ड्	ढ्	ट्	ठ्	ड्	ढ्	
	त्	थ्	द्	ध्	त्	थ्	द्	ध्	
	प्	फ्	ब्	भ्	प्	फ्	ब्	भ्	
	श्				श्				
	ष्				ष्				
	स्				स्				
e.g. मरुत्तम् । पक्षे मरुत् तम् ।									

38 Pratyahara khar

8.4.55 खरि च । When a झल् letter is followed by a खर् letter, then a चर् letter is the replacement for the झल् ।

झल् letter स्थानी m1/1					खर् letter वर्तमाने m7/1					चर् letter आदेश: m1/1				
क्	ख्	ग्	घ्			क्	ख्					क्				
च्	छ्	ज्	झ्			च्	छ्					च्				
ट्	ठ्	ड्	ढ्			ट्	ठ्					ट्				
त्	थ्	द्	ध्			त्	थ्					त्				
प्	फ्	ब्	भ्			प्	फ्					प्				
श्						श्						श्				
ष्						ष्						ष्				
स्						स्						स्				
ह्																

झल् letter + खर् letter => चर् letter + खर् letter ॥

ख्+क्=>क्+क् ॥ ख्+ख्=>क्+ख् ॥

ग्+क्=>क्+क् ॥ ग्+ख्=>क्+ख् ॥ घ्+क्=>क्+क् ॥ घ्+ख्=>क्+ख् ॥

द्+त् =>त्+त् ॥ द्+थ् =>त्+थ् ॥ ध्+त् =>त्+त् ॥ ध्+थ् =>त्+थ् ॥

Notice that some letters in the chart are either redundant or serve no technical usage. E.g. क्+क्=>क्+क् ॥ क्+ख्=>क्+ख् ॥

Some cases in the chart may not be encountered in the language. E.g. ह्+क् ॥ these are what we call boundary conditions or never-used-conditions during computer programming and logic coding.

8.4.54 अभ्यासे चर्च । अभ्यासे चर् च । चर् 1/1

During Reduplication, the झल् letter in the reduplicated syllable is replaced by a corresponding चर् letter OR a corresponding जश् letter as the case may be.

By extrapolation, if the reduplicated झल् letter is a
चर् letter, then it remains unchanged (1st of row and sibilant)
जश् letter, then it remains unchanged (3rd of row)
खँ letter (hard 2nd of row), then replaced by चय् letter (1st of row)
झष् letter (soft 4th of row), then replaced by जश् letter (3rd of row)

झल् letter स्थानी m1/1				चर् letter or जश् letter आदेश: m1/1			Example if reduplicate contains
क्	ख्	ग्	घ्	क्		ग्	क् , ग् no change
च्	छ्	ज्	झ्	च्		ज्	श् , ष् , स् no change
ट्	ठ्	ड्	ढ्	ट्		ड्	ख् changes to क्
त्	थ्	द्	ध्	त्		द्	घ् changes to ग्
प्	फ्	ब्	भ्	प्		ब्	
श्				श्			
ष्				ष्			
स्				स्			
ह्							

e.g. Root खन् + सन् affix iii/1 => ख खन् इट् स ति => चिखनिषति ।
Here a lot of other processing has also taken place, so the example does not clearly explain this.

40 Pratyahara śar

8.3.36 वा शरि । शरि [7/1]

Visarga changes to Visarga Optionally when followed by शर् letter. शर् letters are the sibilants.

e.g. Visarga + शर् => Visarga + शर् । पक्षे सकार + शर् ।

14	ह ल्	अल् , हल् , वल् , रल् , झल् , शल्

1.1.65 अलोऽन्त्यात् पूर्व उपधा । अलः 5/1

In an entity, the अल् letter preceding the final अल् letter is named उपधा penultimate letter.

Pratyahara अल् stands for the entire alphabet.

e.g.

In रामः penultimate is अकार ।

In राम penultimate is आकार ।

In Root भू penultimate is भकार ।

In Root एध् penultimate is एकार ।

In Root इट् penultimate is इकार ।

In Root ईड् penultimate is ईकार ।

Application of this sutra can be seen in 7.3.86 पुगन्तलघूपधस्य च ।
Penultimate short इक् vowel takes Guna.

42 Pratyahara hal

1.1.7 हलोऽनन्तराः संयोगः । हलः ^{1/3}

हकार of Pratyahara हल् is from शिवसूत्र ह य व र ट् ।
Two or more हल् letters that do not have any vowel in them is
named संयोग Conjunct.

Pratyahara हल् stands for all consonants.

43 Pratyahara val

6.1.66 लोपो व्योर्वलि । वलि [7/1]

Pratyahara वल् stands for all consonants except यकार ।

The final वकार and यकार of a Root or Stem are elided when facing a वल् letter.

e.g. Roots Dhatu Serial Number 483 to 488 are all यकार ending. Also these have ई as Tag, so निष्ठा becomes अनिट् ।
ऊय् + क्त affix => ऊय् + त => ऊत + सुँ => ऊतः ।

1.2.26 रलो व्युपधाद्धलादेः संश्च । रलः 5/1

Pratyahara रल् stands for all consonants except य् , व् ।

In the case of consonant beginning Roots that

Have a penultimate इकार or उकार

AND

those that are ending in रल् letter

To such roots, Optionally the सेट् सन् and सेट् क्त्वा affixes behave as अकित्. Since कित् affixes do not cause Guna, purpose of making अकित् is that it will cause Guna.

e.g. Root लिख् + सन् affix => लिलिखिषति । पक्षे लिलेखिषति ।

e.g. Root लिख् + क्त्वा affix => लेखित्वा । पक्षे लिखित्वा ।

45 Pratyahara jhal

8.2.26 झलो झलि । झलः ^{5/1} झलि ^{7/1} ।

Pratyahara झल् means consonants except semi vowels and nasals.

When सकार comes between two झल् letters, it gets dropped.
Here सकार is one that belongs to an affix and the following is an
Affix having an initial झल् letter.

झल् letter वर्तमाने m7/1	सकार of Affix स्थानी m1/1	Affix beginning with झल् letter वर्तमाने m7/1	सकार Elided लोपः m1/1
क् ख् ग् घ् च् छ् ज् झ् ट् ठ् ड् ढ् त् थ् द् ध् प् फ् ब् भ् श् ष् स् ह्	सिँच् of लुङ् i.e. स्	e.g. an atmanepada affix त iii/1	
e.g. Root भिद् + लुङ् iii/1 => अभित्त ।			

46 Pratyahara śal

3.1.45 शल इगुपधादनिटः क्सः । शलः 5/1

Pratyahara शल् means sibilants and aspirate.

For a Root ending in a शल् letter and having an इक् penultimate letter, To such a root in matters of Aorist Past Tense लुङ् लकार , the अनिट् च्लि is replaced by क्स ।

e.g. Root दुह् + लुङ् iii/1=>दुह् + च्लि + त्=>दुह् + क्स + त्=>अधुक्षत् ।

Technical Terms in Grammar

We see some grammatical terms to facilitate our understanding.

Term	Meaning	Stem	Declines like
आगमः	Augment letter	आगम m	राम m
आदेशः	Substitute letter	आदेश m	राम m
इत्	Tag letter = indicatory letter	इत् n	मरुत् n
स्थानी	Substituend letter	स्थानिन् m	करिन् m
वर्तमाने	In presence of condition	वर्तमान m	राम m

Term	Meaning	Remarks
निमित्तः	cause	In presence of condition
प्रत्ययः	Affix	The parasmaipada or atmanepada affixes, etc.
प्रत्याहारः	Array of letters	Abbreviation, Set, Matrix exhibiting some common quality
लोपः	Dropping, elision, disapperance	Invisibl yet exerting influence. A letter that gets dropped after doing its work.
लुक् , श्लु, लुप्	Dropping	context based variations of लोपः
हृ	Aspirate	A soft mahaPrana
ङ ,ञ ,ण ,न ,म	Nasal	called अनुनासिक
कर्कशः , कठोरः	Hard consonant	1st and 2nd of row and sibilants
मृदुः	Soft consonant	3rd and 4th of row, nasals, semi vowels, aspirate

1st, 2nd, 3rd, 4th of row	Sonant	Row consonant except nasal
1st and 2nd of row	Surd	Hard consonant
स्पर्शः	Having contact of tongue. Touching in the mouth to some place.	The 25 row class consonants have the quality of स्पर्शः
अन्तःस्थ	Standing In between	Semi vowels have this quality य् , र् , ल् , व्
ऊष्मः	Hot, having a hissing sound	Sibilants have this quality श् , ष् , स्
अयोगवाह	Made by flow of two letters. Ayogavaha sounds are the Anusvara, Visarga, Ardha visarga and Yama	Ardha Visarga is of two types, Jihvamuliya and Upadhmaniya. Yama is of four types.
जिह्वामूलीय	Jihvamuliya means originating from root of tongue	When visarga faces the hard consonant क् or ख् it is said to become a Jihvamuliya.
उपधमानीय	Upadhmaniya	When visarga faces the hard consonant प् or फ् it is said to become an Upadhmaniya.
अकारः	Traditionally the letters have been named by joining कार	A way of calling or denoting a specific letter of the Alphabet. अकार, इकार, ककार, तकार, सकार , etc.
सन्ध्यक्षरः	Mixed vowel	Diphthongs ए , ऐ , ओ , औ

ह्रस्वः	short	A name for the vowels अ , इ , उ , ऋ , ऌ
दीर्घः	long	A name for the vowels आ , ई , ऊ , ॠ
लघुः	light	Another name for vowels अ , इ , उ , ऋ , ऌ
गुरुः	heavy	A name for Long vowels and diphthongs. Short vowels when followed by a conjunct also get this term.
आनुपूर्वी	Sequence of distinct letters	e.g. राम = र् आ म् अ ।
धातुः	Dhatu means Root	Collection of sounds from the Dhatupatha of Panini
अङ्गः	Anga	An entity that faces another during word construction
प्रातिपदिकम्	Stem	Pratidpadika refers to a noun stem that undergoes some processing to make the final noun
उपदेशः	Whatever has been spoken or taught by Panini.	E.g. the discourses named Ashtadhyayi, Dhatupatha, etc.
आस्यम्	Place of sound in the mouth	e.g. guttural, palatal
प्रयत्नः	Effort in making a sound	e.g. alpaPrana, mahaPrana
अल्पप्राणः	alpaPrana	Unaspirated letter e.g. क्
महाप्राणः	mahaPrana	Aspirated letter e.g. ख्
द्वित्वम्	Doubling of Roots	e.g. Roots of 3c gana जुहोत्यादि undergo doubling
अभ्यासः	In case of	Similarly both portions together

	doubling of a Root, the left side or prior portion is called अभ्यास	of a reduplicated Root are called अभ्यस्त
प्रगृह्यः	Words in dual द्विवचनं ending in ई , ऊ , ए	
अपृक्तः	An affix consisting of a single letter	e.g. the parasmaipada लङ् लकार iii/1 affix त् and ii/1 affix स्
अवसानम्	The last letter of a verse.	The letter that ends in a fullstop. सः ग्रामं गच्छति । Here इकार is called अवसानम्

List of Ashtadhyayi Sutras discussed

1.1.1 वृद्धिरादैच् ।

1.1.3 इको गुणवृद्धी ।

1.1.51 उरण् रपरः ।

बालमनोरमा० अत्र रँ इति प्रत्याहारो विवक्षितः ।

1.1.64 अचोऽन्त्यादि टि ।

1.1.65 अलोऽन्त्यात् पूर्व उपधा ।

1.1.69 अणुदित् सवर्णस्य चाप्रत्ययः ।

1.1.7 हलोऽनन्तराः संयोगः ।

1.2.26 रलो व्युपधाद्धलादेः संश्च ।

3.1.45 शल इगुपधादनिटः क्सः ।

4.1.6 उगितश्च ।

6.1.101 अकः सवर्णे दीर्घः ।

6.1.114 हशि च ।

6.1.66 लोपो व्योर्वलि ।

6.1.77 इको यणचि ।

6.1.78 एचोऽयवायावः ।

6.1.94 एङि पररूपम् ।

6.3.68 इच एकाचोऽम्प्रत्ययवच्च ।

7.2.8 नेड् वशि कृति ।

7.3.101 अतो दीर्घो यञि ।

8.2.26 झलो झलि ।

8.2.37 एकाचो बशो भष् झषन्तस्य स्ध्वोः ।

8.2.37 एकाचो बशो भष् झषन्तस्य स्ध्वोः ।

8.2.39 झलां जशोऽन्ते ।

8.3.17 भोभगोअघोअपूर्वस्य योऽशि ।

8.3.32 ङ्मो ह्रस्वादचि ङ्मुण् नित्यम् ।

8.3.33 मय उञो वो वा ।

8.3.36 वा शरि ।

8.3.57 इण्कोः ।

8.3.6 पुमः खय्यम्परे ।

8.3.7 नश्छव्यप्रशान् । नः छवि अप्रशान् ।

8.4.45 यरोऽनुनासिकेऽनुनासिको वा ।

8.4.48 नादिन्याक्रोशे पुत्रस्य ।

वा० चयो द्वितीयाः शरि पौष्करसादेरिति वाच्यम् ।

8.4.53 झलां जश् झशि ।

8.4.54 अभ्यासे चर्च ।

8.4.55 खरि च ।

8.4.58 अनुस्वारस्य ययि परसवर्णः ।

8.4.62 झयो होऽन्यतरस्याम् ।

8.4.63 शश्छोऽटि ।

8.4.64 हलो यमां यमि लोपः ।

8.4.65 झरो झरि सवर्णे ।

Unadi 1.114 अमन्ताङ् ङः ।

Pronunciation of Sanskrit Letters

उच्चारणम्

अ son आ father इ it ई beat उ full ऊ pool ऋ rhythm

ॠ marine ऌ revelry ॡ ए play ऐ aisle ओ go औ loud

अं Anusvara is pure nasal – close the lips – similar to म्

अः Visarga is Breath release like ह and preceding vowel sound

e.g. Pronounce नमः as नमह , शान्तिः as शान्तिहि , विष्णुः as विष्णुहु

क seeK	ख Khan	ग Get	घ loGHut	ङ sing
च Chunk	छ catchhim	ज Jump	झ heDGEhog	ञ bunch
ट True	ठ anTHill	ड Drum	ढ goDHead	ण under
त Tamil	थ Thunder	द That	ध breaTHE	न nut
प Put	फ Fruit	ब Bin	भ abhor	म much

य loYal र Red ल Luck व Vase श Sure ष Shun स So Hum ह

Conjuncts in general – first utter the top part and then the bottom one, e.g.

Bhagavad Gita 10.16 तिष्ठसि -> ष् ठ ,

Bhagavad Gita 10.23 शङ्करश्चास्मि -> ङ् क , श् च

Specific Conjuncts

ह् ण = ह्ण , ह् न = ह्न , ह् म = ह्म

Utter with emphasis on the chest, first the nasal and then the aspiration, e.g. Brahma = ब्रह्म *Pronounce as **Bramha***

Shiksha Vedanga – Science of Pronunciation

Sanskrit is a language that was orally passed on from generation to generation. There are many sections in the Vedic and later texts that talk about the letters of the alphabet and their proper intonation, enunciation and phonetics शिक्षा ।

Taittiriya Upanishad Shiksha Valli
शीक्षां व्याख्यास्यामः । वर्णः स्वरः । मात्रा बलम् । साम सन्तानः ।
इत्युक्तः शीक्षाध्यायः ॥ १.२ (Chapter 1 Anuvaka 2)

Taittiriya Pratisakhya तैत्तिरीय प्रातिशाख्य
अथ वर्णसमाम्नायः ॥ १॥ (Chapter 1)
स्वराः स्पर्शात् तथा अन्तःस्था ऊष्माणः च अथ दशिंताः ।
विसर्ग_अनुस्वार_ळाः च नासिक्याः पञ्च च उदिताः ॥

Paniniya Shiksha पाणिनीय शिक्षा लघु पाठः / वृद्ध पाठः
आकाशवायुप्रभवः शरीरात् समुच्चरन् वक्त्रमुपैति नादः । १.१

Paniniya Shiksha पाणिनीय शिक्षा श्लोकात्मिका
अथ शिक्षां प्रवक्ष्यामि पाणिनीयं मतं यथा । १.१

The Rigved Pratisakhya ऋग्वेद प्रातिशाख्य and Vajasneyi Pratisakhya वाजसनेयी प्रातिशाख्य are also notable texts on शिक्षा ।

Utter each letter clearly and distinctly, with proper position of the tongue in the mouth. This is the aim of the Shiksha texts. It will take some time to practise and getting used to the correct method of reading a Sanskrit letter and text. However it is most rewarding, as our anatomy, bones and muscles are all connected to sound, the key aspect of the fundamental element space.

Place & Effort of Enunciation

Place of speech	Vowels स्वर		Row Consonants व्यञ्जन					Semi vowel	Sibilant
			Alpaprana		Mahaprana				
	Short	Long	1st	2nd	3rd	4th	5th		
कण्ठ	अ	आ	क	ख	ग	घ	ङ		
तालु	इ	ई	च	छ	ज	झ	ञ	य	श
मूर्धा	ऋ	ॠ	ट	ठ	ड	ढ	ण	र	ष
दन्त	ऌ		त	थ	द	ध	न	ल	स
ओष्ठ	उ	ऊ	प	फ	ब	भ	म		
Consonants are supplied with vowel अ to aid enunciation									

कण्ठ – तालु	ए	ऐ	Diphthongs have twin places of utterance, being compound vowels
कण्ठ – ओष्ठ	ओ	औ	
दन्त – ओष्ठ	व		The vakara is different from the other semivowels as it has twin places of utterance
नासिक्य	ः , अं		Anusvara is a pure Nasal
अनुनासिका	ँ , ॐ , यँ		Candrabindu means Nasalization

कण्ठ Soft, Mahaprana	ह	Hakara is an Aspirate. It is sounded like a soft release of breath
	◌ः	Visarga is an Aspirate. It is sounded like ह alongwith its preceding vowel

Ardha Visarga ◌ः is also written as ✕		
Base of tongue Hard, Alpaprana	◌ः or ✕	Jihvamuliya pronounce as ह् (a visarga preceding क , ख)
ओष्ठ Hard, Alpaprana	◌ः or ✕ or ꣳ	Upadhmaniya pronounce as फ् (a visarga preceding प , फ)

कण्ठ्य Guttural or Velar	तालव्य Palatal	मूर्धन्य Cerebral or Retroflex or Lingual	दन्त्य Dental	ओष्ठ्य Labial

All vowels and semi vowels are termed voiced घोष वर्ण । This means that a background sound is produced from the tremor in the vocal cords in addition to the active sound produced in speaking. The 3rd, 4th and 5th letters of the row class consonants are also घोष वर्ण ।

The 1st and 2nd letters of the row class consonants, the sibilants and the aspirate are termed अघोष वर्ण । This means that no background sound arises from the tremor in the vocal cords.

All row consonants are termed स्पर्श वर्ण Tongue makes contact

The unit of time for enunication is a short vowel, having 1 matra.
The long vowels and diphthongs have 2 matras.
A consonant has only ½ matra and it is supplied with a vowel for proper enunciation.

VOWELS स्वर

>Long Vowels are sounded twice as long as the short vowels.
>DIPHTHONGS सन्ध्यक्षर (सन्धि – अक्षर) Are combinations of two vowels and are sounded long.

GUTTURALS कण्ठ्य (also known as VELAR)

>Sounded from the throat with the tongue resting.

PALATALS तालव्य

>Sounded with the tongue raised slightly.

CEREBRALS मूर्धन्य (also known as RETROFLEX or LINGUAL)

>Sounded with the tongue touching the roof of the mouth.

DENTALS दन्त्य

>Sounded with the tongue distinctly touching the teeth.

LABIALS ओष्ठ्य

>Sounded with the lips distinctly touching each other.

Devanagari Latin ISO 15919 Chart

अ	आ	इ	ई	उ	ऊ	ऋ	ॠ	ऌ	
a	ā	i	ī	u	ū	ṛ	ṝ	ḷ	
						◌	◌	◌	
ए	ऐ	ओ	औ	◌̇	◌̃	◌:		✕	
ē	ai	ō	au	ṁ	m̐	ḥ		Ardha visarga	

Consonants are shown with vowel a = अ for uttering							
क	ख	ग	घ	ङ	Consonant only with halant		
ka	kha	ga	gha	ṅa	क्अ = क		ka
च	छ	ज	झ	ञ		क्	k
ca	cha	ja	jha	ña	Halant ◌ is not a separate
ट	ठ	ड	ढ	ण	character in the transliteration.
ṭa	ṭha	ḍa	ḍha	ṇa	It simply means lack of vowel in the consonant.
त	थ	द	ध	न	e.g. Both these words end in "n"
ta	tha	da	dha	na	but one has a halant in
प	फ	ब	भ	म	Devanagari. So the word without
pa	pha	ba	bha	ma	the halant has a vowel added to it in transliteration. E.g. Arjuna
य	र	ल	व		अर्जुन śrī bhagavān श्री भगवान्
ya	ra	la	va		
श	ष	स	ह		ळ	ऽ	avagraha
śa	ṣa	sa	ha		ḻa	'	

The ISO 15919 standard
http://www.iso.org/iso/iso_catalogue/catalogue_tc/catalogue_det
ail.htm?csnumber=28333

References

Author	Title	Year	Ed	Publisher
V S Apte	संस्कृत हिन्दी कोश (1890 Ed)	1997	1st	Oriental Book Center, Delhi
C. C. Uhlenbeck	A Manual of Sanskrit Phonetics	1898	1st	Uhlenbeck, London
Charudev Shastri	व्याकरण महाभाष्य प्रथम नवाह्निक	1968	1st	Motilal Banarsidass, Delhi
Shivraj Acharya Kondinyayan	पाणिनीय शिक्षा	2012	1st	Chaukhamba Surbharti Prakashan, Varanasi
Satyanand Vedvagish	पाणिनीय त्रिपाठी पाणिनिमुनिप्रोक्त पाठानां सोदाहरणः सङ्ग्रहः	2013	1st	Satyanand Vedvagish, Arya Samaj Gandhidham
Brahmadutt Jignasu	अष्टाध्यायी भाष्य प्रथमावृत्ति Vol 1-2-3	2013	7th	Ramlal Kapoor Trust, Sonipat
Sudarshan Dev Acharya	पाणिनीय अष्टाध्यायी प्रवचनम् आर्यभाषा नामक हिन्दी टीका Vol1 (Reprint of 1997 Ed)	2014	1st	Shrimad Dayanand Vedarsh Mahavidyalaya Nyas
Somlekha	पाणिनीय शिक्षा	2014	1st	Chaukhamba Sanskrit Pratishthan, Delhi
Yudhisthir Mimamsak	शिक्षा सूत्राणि	2014	1st	Ram Lal Kapoor Trust, Sonipat
Govindacharya, Lakshmi Sharma	वैयाकरणसिद्धान्तकौमुदी 'श्रीधरमुखोल्हासिनी' हिन्दीव्याख्यासमन्विता - प्रारम्भ से अव्ययान्त Vol1	2016	1st	Chaukhamba Surbharti Prakashan, Varanasi
S C Vasu, Vinod Kumar	The Ashtadhyayi of Panini Vol 1-2	2017	1st	Parimal Publication, Delhi

	The Sanskrit Alphabet	2017	1st	Devotees of Sri Sri Ravi Shankar Ashram, Punjab
Ashwini Kumar Aggarwal	Dhatupatha Verbs in 5 Lakaras Vol3: Relevant Ashtadhyayi Sutras, Vartikas, Karikas, GanaSutras, Tags & Indexes	2017	1st	

Papers

1. Paul Kiparsky: Economy and the Construction of the Sivasutras, Stanford University
2. Wiebke Petersen: A Mathematical Analysis of Panini's Sivasutras: Journal of Logic, Language and Information 13:471-479, 2004
3. Wiebke Petersen, Silke Hamann: On the generalizability of Panini's pratyahara-technique to other languages. Heinrich-Heine University, Düsseldorf 2010
4. Andras Kornai: The generative power of feature geometry. CLSI, Stanford University

From the Net

http://spokensanskrit.org/

Audio Learning

Vyoma Linguistics Labs Foundation, Bangalore https://vyomalabs.in/

ॐ

Epilogue

Everything in creation is made up of space and sound is an attribute of space. The Maheshwar Sutra is one of the earliest attempts of mankind to establish the Science of Sounds in a a mathematical, precise and logical manner.

सर्वे भवन्तु सुखिनः । सर्वे सन्तु निरामयाः ।

सर्वे भद्राणि पश्यन्तु । मा कश्चिद् दुःख भाग् भवेत् ॥

ॐ शान्तिः शान्तिः शान्तिः

When faith has blossomed in life, Every step is led by the Divine.

Sri Sri Ravi Shankar

Om Namah Shivaya

जय गुरुदेव

Made in the USA
Las Vegas, NV
28 January 2022

42451292R00066